SAP® MM

Questions and Answers

SAP® MM

Questions and Answers

Kogent Learning Solutions, Inc.

JONES AND BARTLETT PUBLISHERS
Sudbury, Massachusetts
BOSTON   TORONTO   LONDON   SINGAPORE

World Headquarters

Jones and Bartlett Publishers
40 Tall Pine Drive
Sudbury, MA 01776
978-443-5000
info@jbpub.com
www.jbpub.com

Jones and Bartlett Publishers
Canada
6339 Ormindale Way
Mississauga, Ontario L5V 1J2
Canada

Jones and Bartlett Publishers
International
Barb House, Barb Mews
London W6 7PA
United Kingdom

Jones and Bartlett's books and products are available through most bookstores and online booksellers. To contact Jones and Bartlett Publishers directly, call 800-832-0034, fax 978-443-8000, or visit our website www.jbpub.com.

Substantial discounts on bulk quantities of Jones and Bartlett's publications are available to corporations, professional associations, and other qualified organizations. For details and specific discount information, contact the special sales department at Jones and Bartlett via the above contact information or send an email to specialsales@jbpub.com.

Production Credits

Publisher: David Pallai
Editorial Assistant: Molly Whitman
Production Assistant: Ashlee Hazeltine
Senior Marketing Manager: Andrea DeFronzo
Associate Marketing Manager: Lindsay Ruggiero
V.P., Manufacturing and Inventory Control:
  Therese Connell

Composition: diacriTech
Art Rendering: diacriTech
Cover and Title Page Design: Scott Moden
Cover Image: © kentoh/ShutterStock, Inc.
Printing and Binding: Malloy, Inc.
Cover Printing: Malloy, Inc.

Library of Congress Cataloging-in-Publication Data

SAP MM questions and answers/Kogent Learning Solutions, Inc.
    p. cm.
  Includes index.
  ISBN-13: 978-0-7637-8144-6 (pbk.)
  ISBN-10: 0-7637-8144-4 (ibid.)
  1. SAP ERP. 2. Integrated software 3. Materials management. I. Kogent Learning Solutions, Inc.
  QA76.76.157S257 2010
  004'.36–dc22

                                2009023558

6048
Printed in the United States of America
13 12 11 10 09   10 9 8 7 6 5 4 3 2 1

TRADEMARK ACKNOWLEDGMENT

This publication contains references to the products of SAP AG. SAP, R/3, xApps, xApp, SAP NetWeaver, Duet, PartnerEdge, ByDesign, SAP Business ByDesign, and other SAP products and services mentioned herein are trademarks or registered trademarks of SAP AG in Germany and in several other countries all over the world.

Business Objects and the Business Objects logo, BusinessObjects, Crystal Reports, Crystal Decisions, Web Intelligence, Xcelsius and other Business Objects products and services mentioned herein are trademarks or registered trademarks of Business Objects in the United States and/or other countries.

SAP AG is neither the author nor the publisher of this publication and is not responsible for its content, and SAP Group shall not be liable for errors or omissions with respect to the materials.

TABLE OF CONTENTS

Introduction   *ix*

Chapter 1   Introduction to SAP Materials Management   1

Chapter 2   Organizational Structure   13

Chapter 3   Master Data   25

Chapter 4   Procurement and Purchasing   75

Chapter 5   Materials Requirement Planning   141

Chapter 6   Inventory Management   165

Chapter 7   Logistics Invoice Verification   199

Chapter 8   Valuation and Account Assignment   221

Chapter 9   Release Procedures   233

                 Glossary   241

                 Question Index   247

INTRODUCTION

Congratulations on your purchase of *SAP® MM Questions and Answers*! This book acts as a comprehensive guide for students and professionals who intend to learn more about SAP Materials Management (SAP MM). It is often difficult to find a book that gives an overview of important topics and also contains valuable concepts that are frequently asked on SAP certification exams. Such a frenetic search normally consumes a lot of time and energy, as you need to explore huge numbers of books on the MM module, one of the core modules in the SAP® system. We present *SAP® MM Questions and Answers* as a one-stop solution to your search for a quality book focusing on probable interview questions on SAP MM.

This book covers all the useful content necessary to clinch an interview. It is compiled in an easy-to-understand and self-explanatory manner. Through this book, you will gain a quick understanding of the MM module and its in-depth features. The book explores the following topics:

- A brief introduction to SAP technology, its history, a list of other enterprise resource planning (ERP) applications available in the market, an explanation of the ERP application, mySAP™ ERP, and a list of different modules of SAP® R/3®.

- The organizational structure of the MM module and the concepts of clients, companies, plants, storage locations, purchasing organizations, and purchase groups.

- The importance of master data in the MM module, the different types of master data, and concepts related to the material master, vendor master, and inventory master.

- Procurement and purchasing concepts such as special procurement types, consignment stock, special stock, and subcontracting, as well as the complete cycle of procurement, from determining the requirements to processing the payments.

- Materials requirement planning (MRP), including its types and procedures, consumption-based planning, different models of forecasting, and the concepts of total planning and planned orders.

- The management of inventory in the SAP system, including management of different goods movements such as goods receipt, goods issue, stock transfer, and transfer posting.

- The concept of logistics invoice verification (LIV) and its features, the invoice verification process, evaluated receipt settlements (ERS), parked invoice documents, and the procedures to post an invoice.

- The purpose of material valuation, factors controlling material valuation, valuation class, valuation area, balance sheet valuations, and Last In, First Out (LIFO) and First In, First Out (FIFO) valuations.

- The concepts of release procedure, release criterion, release code, release group, and release strategy.

CHAPTER 1
INTRODUCTION TO SAP MATERIALS MANAGEMENT

Introduction to SAP Materials Management

1. What is SAP? How is it used in industries?

- SAP is the most popular enterprise resource planning (ERP) software application used to provide enterprise business solutions. It was first introduced in 1972 in Mannheim, Germany. SAP stands for Systems, Applications, and Products in Data Processing.

- SAP provides complete business solutions by integrating various business tasks such as sales, purchase, and production. SAP takes information from one business process and incorporates it into another business process, thereby speeding up all business processes. For example, information about the raw material in stock is used by the production department to determine how to prepare products.

- SAP is widely used in various industries because as it updates and processes important data very quickly, it can automate business processes and provide real-time solutions for businesses.

2. Briefly describe the history of the SAP software.

- The SAP software was developed by a company of the same name. SAP (the company) was founded in 1972 by five former IBM employees: Dietmar Hopp, Hans-Werner Hector,

Hasso Plattner, Klaus Tschira, and Claus Wellenreuther. SAP released its mainframe product, called SAP R/2, in 1979. The client/server version of the SAP software, called SAP R/3, was released in 1992. Today, SAP is the largest vendor of standard business-application software. SAP constantly delivers scalable solutions to its customers, allowing them to respond to dynamic market conditions and helping them to maintain an advantage over their competitors. Some of the major SAP applications presently available are defined in question 4 and include SAP R/3, mySAP ERP, mySAP Customer Relationship Management (CRM), mySAP Supplier Relationship Management (SRM), mySAP Supply Chain Management (SCM), and mySAP Product Lifecycle Management (PLM), to name a few.

3.   **Why is SAP so popular? What are some of the other ERP applications available in the market?**

- SAP is the most popular ERP software available because it updates and processes business data in real time. Available ERP software can be divided into two categories: open-source ERP software and proprietary ERP software. Some of the most commonly used ERP applications are listed in the following table.

Open-Source ERP Software	Proprietary ERP Software
Adempiere	1C:Enterprise (1C Company)
BlueErp	24 SevenOffice (24 SevenOffice)
Compiere	Accpac (Sage Group)
Dollibar	BatchMaster ERP (BatchMaster Software)
ERPS	Epicor Enterprise (Epicor)
JFire	Microsoft Dynamics AX (Microsoft)
OpenERP	JD Edwards EnterpriseOne (Oracle)
OrangeHRM	E-Business Suit (Oracle)
SQL-Ledger	PeopleSoft (Oracle)

Open-Source ERP Software	Proprietary ERP Software
WebERP	Siebel CRM (Oracle)
Postbooks	IFS Applications
Opentaps	Ramco Ondemand ERP (Ramco Systems)

4.   What is mySAP ERP? What business components can it be classified into?

- mySAP ERP is the next-generation ERP application from SAP AG in Germany, and was first launched in 2003. The mySAP ERP application has all the features of previously released SAP ERP software, such as SAP R/3 and SAP Strategic Enterprise Management (SEM), along with its own extensions. The mySAP ERP application provides e-commerce solutions by using Web technology. The mySAP ERP application has the following advantages:
  - Mobile infrastructure, which improves workforce mobility
  - Transparency through a business intelligence framework
  - Delivery of people-centric services
  - Faster access to information, which facilitates quick decision making
  - Seamless integration of processes throughout the business
- mySAP ERP includes the following products:
  - mySAP Enterprise Resource Planning (ERP)
  - mySAP Supply Chain Management (SCM)
  - mySAP Supplier Relationship Management (SRM)
  - mySAP Customer Relationship Management (CRM)
  - mySAP Product Life Cycle Management (PLM)
- mySAP R/3 can be classified into the following business components:
  - Financial applications
  - Human resource applications

- ☐ Logistics
- ☐ Sales and distribution applications

5.   What are the industry-specific solutions available in mySAP?

- ■ The mySAP ERP application provides business solutions for almost every industry, including automotive, chemical, and media. Various industry-specific solutions available in mySAP include the following:
  - ☐ mySAP Automotive
  - ☐ mySAP Aerospace and Defense
  - ☐ mySAP Consumer Products
  - ☐ mySAP Banking
  - ☐ mySAP Chemicals
  - ☐ mySAP High Tech
  - ☐ mySAP Engineering and Construction
  - ☐ mySAP Healthcare
  - ☐ mySAP Higher Education and Research
  - ☐ mySAP Insurance
  - ☐ mySAP Media
  - ☐ mySAP Oil and Gas
  - ☐ mySAP Mill Products
  - ☐ mySAP Mining
  - ☐ mySAP Public Sector
  - ☐ mySAP Pharmaceuticals
  - ☐ mySAP Service Providers
  - ☐ mySAP Retail
  - ☐ mySAP Telecommunications
  - ☐ mySAP Utilities

6.   What is SAP R/3?

- ■ SAP R/3 is an ERP software that was officially launched in 1992. It is a replacement for the SAP R/2 mainframe computing-based ERP software and is based on client-server computing. With the advent of client-server computing, SAP AG in Germany (founder of the SAP ERP software) launched SAP R/3 to provide client-server-based real-time business solutions. The letter "R" in SAP R/3 represents the real-time business data processing, while the number "3" represents the three tiers in client-server computing.

■ The three tiers in client-server computing are: presentation (client), application (business logic), and database (stores the actual business data).

■ SAP R/3 integrates various business areas, such as sales, purchase, and procurement, by using different functional modules, such as Materials Management (MM), Sales and Distribution (SD), Financial (FI), Controlling (CO), and Human Resource (HR).

■ Different versions of SAP R/3 include 3.1i, 4.0b, 4.5b, 4.6b, and 4.6c; the latest version is 4.70.

7. How did different versions of SAP evolve?

■ Since its inception, SAP has continued to support changing business processes and to adapt itself to the needs of organizations. In order to support the most current business strategies, SAP has evolved over time and progressed through the following versions:

☐ SAP R/1—This was the first version of SAP and was developed for financial accounting systems. This version is no longer available.

☐ SAP R/2—This was the second version of SAP. It replaced the R/1 version in the 1970s and was a mainframe-based business application. SAP R/2 supported multiple currencies and languages to help internationalize business management. This version is also no longer available.

☐ SAP R/3—This version replaced SAP R/2, adding support for client-server-based distributed systems. This new version of SAP is multi-platformed, meaning it can be installed and used on multiple platforms, such as Windows or UNIX.

8. Why are industry-specific solutions used in SAP R/3?

■ Industry-specific solutions are used in the SAP R/3 ERP application in order to automate various business processes for almost every industry, including automotive, oil and gas, and chemical. By automating business processes, the SAP R/3 application helps organizations meet the following challenges:

- ☐ *Emerging markets*—Earning revenue in emerging markets
- ☐ *Competition*—Maintaining successful business operations in a world of fierce competition
- ☐ *Increasing demands*—Handling increasing and varying customer demands
- ☐ *Labor issues*—Solving the problems that arise for business operations requiring efficient skilled labor
- ☐ *Workforce shortages*—Solving the problem of a shortage of skilled personnel

■ The importance of industry-specific solutions comes from a very basic foundation of thought: every type of business is unique and therefore needs to be catered to accordingly. The same philosophy may not be applicable for automotive businesses and integrated steel plants, because both require entirely different approaches to business planning. The automotive industry is based on the assembling of equipment and parts–discrete manufacturing, whereas the integrated steel plant is a continuous manufacturing unit. Therefore, each business's functionalities are different in areas such as production and inventory management.

9. What benefits will be realized after implementing SAP in any organization?

■ After the installation of SAP R/3 in an organization, the following changes will occur:

- ☐ Improvement in project management and project execution capabilities
- ☐ Integration of suppliers and subcontractors
- ☐ Optimization of sales-order capabilities
- ☐ Comprehensive business support specific to a particular industry type
- ☐ Minimal cost of ownership
- ☐ Uniformity of business processes
- ☐ Ability to make safe strategic choices

10. What are the different modules in SAP R/3?

■ To integrate various business processes, SAP R/3 comes with various modules, such as MM, SD, and CO. These modules are further grouped into various business-functional areas. The functional areas and the SAP R/3 modules in those functional areas are as follows:

  □ *Financial applications*—Deals with an organization's financial matters, such as preparing and analyzing financial documents and reporting the document output to the appropriate authorities for further processing. To manage all these concerns, the following SAP R/3 modules are grouped in this functional area:

   ▪ FI—Financial Accounting

   ▪ CO—Controlling

   ▪ EC—Enterprise Controlling

   ▪ IM—Investment Management

   ▪ TR—Treasury

  □ *Human resources*—Deals with documents related to an organization's human resources department. The SAP R/3 modules grouped in this area help an organization to manage processes such as salary creation and distribution, employees' payroll across the organization, and transferring data to other relevant departments, such as finance. This area consists of the following modules:

   ▪ Personnel Management

   ▪ Time Management

   ▪ Payroll

   ▪ Training and Event Management

   ▪ Organizational Management

  □ *Logistics applications*—This is the largest area covered by SAP R/3. This area helps manage broad-level business processes such as sales and distribution of products, materials management, production planning, and quality management. This area consists of the following modules:

   ▪ MM—Materials Management

   ▪ SD—Sales and Distribution

   ▪ PP—Production Planning

- PM—Plant Maintenance
- LO—Logistics
- QM—Quality Management
- PS—Project System
- WM—Warehouse Management

11.   What are the core functionalities of the SAP system?

- The core functionalities of the SAP system are Sales and Distribution (SD), Materials Management (MM), Financial Accounting (FI), and Production Planning (PP). In the first phase, companies implement the SAP software with these core functionalities. Later, in the second and third phases, they may also introduce other functionalities, such as Controlling (CO), Warehouse Management (WM), and Human Resource (HR). However, the types of modules and the phasing of implementation depends solely on the type of industry in which the client works, as well as the organization's readiness and the urgency with which the integrated enterprise system, such as SAP, must be adopted.

12.   How can we define an MM module? What is its importance in SAP R/3?

- MM stands for Materials Management and is a part of the Logistics functional area of SAP R/3. It is an important SAP R/3 module because it helps manage broad-level business activities, such as procurement, valuation and assignment, batch management, and materials storage. Since materials are the most precious resource of an organization, extreme care needs to be taken in all the processes related to materials management. Efficient materials management is the essence of the MM module of SAP R/3.

13.   How is the MM module integrated with other modules of SAP?

- The MM module deals with materials procurement on the basis of the production required; therefore, it is linked with the PP module.

■ The SD module is proportionally related to the MM module, because it uses information about the quantity of material sent for production.

■ The WM module is related to the MM module, because the MM module maintains information about materials storage and materials transfers inside an organization.

■ The FI module is also related to the MM module, because every operation performed in the MM module directly impacts the financial processes of the organization.

14.   What are the main components of the MM module? How are these components used in SAP?

■ The MM module of SAP R/3 is used for materials procurement and management. This is the largest of all the SAP modules and is divided into the following subcomponents:

☐ *Purchasing*—Allows users to control the entire purchasing process.

☐ *Inventory management*—Allows users to keep track of the materials in stock. It also helps users to perform operations, such as goods receipts, goods issues, and physical stock transfers.

☐ *Invoice verification*—Allows users to verify invoices from vendors. The invoices are compared with the purchase order and the goods receipts in the following three ways:

  ▪ Content

  ▪ Price

  ▪ Quantity

☐ *Physical inventory*—Allows users to keep track of the materials stored in an organization. Inventory is taken on the basis of measurement units, such as number or weight of items, at a given storage location at a specific time.

☐ *Valuation*—Allows users to calculate the value of all fixed and current assets, along with all payables, at a certain time and with the appropriate legal requirements.

☐ *Materials requirements planning*—Helps users to create a materials procurement plan for a plant or company.

□ *Materials master*—Helps users to manage all of the materials-related data.

□ *Service master*—Helps an organization keep records of the services that it procures.

□ *Foreign trade/customs*—Allows users to manage the export and import of merchandise among different customs territories.

CHAPTER 2
ORGANIZATIONAL STRUCTURE

ORGANIZATIONAL STRUCTURE

1. What is the organizational structure in the materials management (MM) module?

■ The organizational structure in the MM module is a hierarchy in which various organizational units are arranged according to their tasks and functions. The different organizational units that constitute the organizational structure of the company are as follows:

  □ *Client*—A self-contained unit in the SAP system with separate master records and its own set of tables.

  □ *Company code*—The smallest organizational unit. You can create an independent set of accounts for this unit for the purpose of external reporting.

  □ *Plant*—An organizational unit where materials are produced or goods and services are provided. You can divide an enterprise into various plants according to production, procurement, maintenance, and materials planning.

  □ *Storage location*—An organizational unit where the goods produced in the plant are stored.

  □ *Warehouse number*—An alphanumeric key that represents a warehousing system, which is made up of different organizational and technical storage areas.

□ *Storage type*—An area such as a goods receipt area, goods issue area, or picking area. Also the physical or logical division of a complex warehouse.

□ *Purchasing organization*—An organizational unit that procures materials and services and negotiates with vendors to purchase materials or goods.

□ *Purchasing group*—An alphanumeric key for a buyer or a group of buyers who are involved in purchasing activities. The purchasing group is responsible for materials procurement and dealing with vendors.

2.   What are the levels of organizational units in Enterprise Structure in SAP R/3?

■ The client is the highest level unit of the organizational units in Enterprise Structure in SAP R/3. The client is followed by the company code, which represents a unit with its own accounting, balance, and profit and loss (P&L). The next level of organizational units in Enterprise Structure is the plant, which represents an operational unit of a company.

3.   Define "client." What is its importance in SAP?

■ A client can be defined as a person, company, or organization that purchases goods from another person, company, or organization. In terms of SAP, a client is defined as a unit that has its own master records and a set of tables. The client is important in SAP because it stores and maintains data about the organization where SAP is implemented.

4.   How do we create a client in the MM module?

■ You can create a client in the MM module either by using the transaction code SCC4 or by performing the following steps:

□ Select *SAP Menu > Tools > Administration > Administration > Client Administration*.

□ Double click *SCC4–Client Maintenance*. The display view *Clients: Overview* screen appears.

□ Select *Display* > *Change*. The information dialog box appears.

□ Click Continue. The change view Clients: Overview screen appears, where you can create a new client.

5.   Define "company." How is it different from a client? What are the data in the MM module that are maintained at the company code level?

■ A company is an organizational unit for which individual financial statements are drawn per the relevant commercial laws. A company consists of one or more company codes. Within a company, all company codes must use the same transactions in addition to the same fiscal year breakdown; however, company code currencies can vary.

■ A company is different from a client because a client can itself be a company, or an organization that has multiple companies. For example, the owner of the entire SAP system is a client. The system will have only one operational client, but the client may further have a group of companies. The following data are held at the company code level:

□ Material number

□ Classification data

□ Multilingual description

□ Units of measure

□ Technical data

6.   How do we create a company code in SAP?

■ In SAP, a company code is created using the transaction OX02. The company code field is represented by a four-character alphanumeric string. You can create a company code in SAP by performing the following steps:

□ Open the SAP Customizing Implementation guide.

□ Select *Enterprise Structure* > *Definition* > *Financial Accounting* > *Edit, Copy, Delete, Check Company Code*. The Choose Activity dialog box appears.

☐ Double-click *Edit Company Code Data*. The change view *Company Code: Overview* screen appears, where you can create a company code.

7. How do we assign a company code to a company in SAP?

■ You can assign a company code to a company by performing the following steps:

☐ Open the SAP Customizing Implementation guide.

☐ Select *Enterprise Structure > Assignment > Financial Accounting > Assign Company Code to Company*. The change view *Assign Company Code > Company: Overview* screen appears, where you can assign a company code to a company.

8. How many charts of accounts can be assigned to a company?

■ You can assign only one chart of accounts to each company.

9. How many company codes can be assigned to one chart of accounts?

■ You can assign many company codes to a chart of accounts.

10. How many company codes can be assigned to a company?

■ You can assign one or more company codes to a company.

11. What is a plant in the MM module?

■ A plant is an organizational unit where materials are produced or goods and services are provided. In SAP, a plant is represented by a unique four-digit alphanumeric number.

A plant is allocated to one company code, and a company can have many plants. In the organizational unit, a plant can be at one of the following locations:

- ☐ Corporate headquarters
- ☐ Central delivery warehouse
- ☐ Manufacturing facility
- ☐ Regional sales office

12. How is a plant defined in the MM module?

■ You can define a plant in the MM by performing the following steps:

- ☐ Select *IMG > Enterprise Structure > Definition > Logistic–General > Define, Copy, Delete, Check Plant.*
- ☐ Click *Execute.* The *Choose Activity* dialog box appears.
- ☐ Select *Define Plant* to create a plant. The change view *Plants: Overview* screen appears.
- ☐ Click *New Entries.* The *New Entries: Details of Added Entries* screen appears.
- ☐ Specify the plant code in the plant field.
- ☐ Click the address icon to display the Edit Address field.
- ☐ Specify the required values in the fields, such as Title, Name, and Search Term 1/2.
- ☐ Click OK. The *New Entries: Details of Added Entries* screen appears again.
- ☐ Click the Save icon to save the newly defined plant.

13. What are the prerequisites for creating a plant?

■ There are three prerequisites that are required in order to create a plant. They are as follows:

- ☐ *Company calendar*—Comprised of work days, public holidays, and company holidays. Every SAP system is provided with a company calendar that can be modified per the schedule of the company.
- ☐ *Country key*—Helps in defining a plant.

☐ *Region key*—Refers to a state or province that is associated with the country. It is required along with the country key.

14. How many company codes can be assigned to a plant?

■ You can assign only one company code to a plant.

15. Can a company code be assigned to many plants?

■ Yes, you can assign one company code to many plants.

16. What is the menu path to assign a company code to a plant?

■ You can assign a company code to a plant by navigating the following menu path: *SAP Menu > Tools > Customizing > IMG > Execute Project > Display IMG (SAP reference IMG) > Enterprise Structure > Assignment > Logistics-General > Assign Company Code to Plant.*

17. What is a storage location in SAP?

■ In the SAP system, a storage location is the place within the premises of a plant where you can store a stock of goods. Each plant has at least one storage location assigned to it.

18. How is a storage location defined in SAP?

■ A storage location is defined by performing the following steps:

☐ Select *Tools > Customizing > SAP Reference IMG > Edit Project.*

☐ Select *Enterprise Structure > Definition > Materials Management > Maintain Storage.*

☐ Click the clock icon (⊕). The *Determine Work Area: Entry* dialog box appears.

☐ Specify the value (P001) for the plant in the dialog box.

- ☐ Click the check mark icon (✔). The change view Storage Locations: Overview screen appears.

- ☐ Click *New Entries*. The *New Entries: Details of Added Entries* screen appears.

- ☐ Specify the value of the storage location and description fields.

- ☐ Click the Save icon to save the storage location.

- ☐ Click the Exit icon to create the storage location.

19.   How is a storage location assigned to a plant?

- ■ You can assign a storage location to a plant either by using the transaction code OX09 or by performing the following steps:

  - ☐ Open the SAP Customizing Implementation guide.

  - ☐ Select *Enterprise Structure > Definition > Materials Management > Maintain Storage Location*. The view cluster *Maintenance: Initial Screen* window appears with the *Determine Work Area: Entry* dialog box opened.

- ■ In the *Determine Work Area: Entry* dialog box, enter a plant number and click Continue. The change view *Storage Locations: Overview* screen appears, where you can assign a storage location to the plant.

20.   Can storage locations be created automatically?

- ■ Storage locations can be created automatically when an inward goods movement for a material is performed. In order to create a storage location automatically, open the SAP Implementation guide and click *Materials Management > Inventory Management and Physical Inventory > Goods Receipt > Create Storage Location Automatically*.

21.   Can two plants have a common storage location?

- ■ A storage location is a unique four-character alphanumeric key; therefore, two plants cannot have a common storage location.

22. What is the menu path to configure the storage location?

■ You can configure the storage location by navigating the following menu path: *Display IMG > Enterprise Structure > Definition > Maintain Storage Location.*

23. What is a purchasing organization in SAP?

■ A purchasing organization can be defined as an organization that negotiates conditions with vendors to purchase goods, materials, or services, and procures said materials and services. Possible forms of a purchasing organization include:

 □ *Enterprise-wide*—One purchasing organization procures materials and services for the whole organization.

 □ *Company-specific*—The purchasing organization is company-specific, that is, one purchasing organization is assigned to and procures materials for one company code in an organization.

 □ *Plant-specific*—One purchasing organization is assigned to and procures materials and services for one plant in an organization.

24. What are the different ways of organizing purchasing organizations?

■ There are two different ways to organize purchasing organizations: distributed purchasing and centralized purchasing. Distributed purchasing means there are multiple purchasing organizations per plant. Centralized purchasing means there is one purchasing organization per plant.

25. How is a purchasing organization defined in SAP?

■ A purchasing organization is defined by performing the following steps:

 □ Select *Tools > Customizing > SAP Reference IMG > Edit Project.*

☐ Select *Enterprise Structure > Definition > Materials Management > Maintain Purchasing Organization.*

☐ Click the clock icon (⊕). The change view *Purchasing Organizations: Overview* screen appears.

☐ Click New Entries. The *New Entries: Details of Added Entries* screen appears.

☐ Specify the value of the purchase organization and purchase organization description fields.

☐ Click the Save icon to save the purchase organization.

☐ Click the Exit icon to create the purchasing organization.

26. What is the reference purchasing organization in SAP?

■ The reference purchasing organization can be defined as an organization whose conditions or contracts are linked to other purchasing organizations. This organization can make conditions or contracts that can easily be used in other purchasing organizations.

27. How is a purchase group defined in SAP?

■ A purchase group is defined by performing the following steps:

☐ Select *Tools > Customizing > SAP Reference IMG > Edit Project.*

☐ Select *Materials Management > Purchasing > Create Purchasing Groups.*

☐ Click the clock icon (⊕). The change view *Purchasing Groups: Overview* screen appears.

☐ Click New Entries to create a purchasing group. The *New Entries: Details of Added Entries* screen appears.

☐ Specify the value of the purchasing group and description fields.

☐ Click the Save icon to save the purchasing group.

☐ Click the Exit icon to create the purchase group.

CHAPTER 3
MASTER DATA

MASTER DATA

1. What is master data in the materials management (MM) module?

■ The master data in the MM module acts as reference data, defining various business entities and playing a key role in the core operation of the business.

2. How is master data important in the MM module?

■ The master data in the MM module contains all of the basic information needed to manage material. The data is stored and sorted on the basis of different criteria, such as the descriptive nature of the material (size, dimension, and weight) and the control functions of the material (material type and industry sector). Apart from data maintained by the user, the master data also stores data that is automatically updated by the system (such as stock levels).

3. What are the various types of master data in the MM module?

■ The different types of master data in the MM module are as follows:
  □ Material master
  □ Vendor master

☐ Purchasing information record

☐ Source list

☐ Quota arrangement

4.   What is a material master file?

■ A material master file stores and maintains all of the information related to managing a material. The material master is sorted on the basis of different criteria.

5.   Why are material master records used in SAP?

■ Material master records are used in the SAP R/3 system to manage material-specific data. The material information stored in material master records is used by all logistics areas in the SAP R/3 system. The material master records integrate all material-specific data into a single database object that eliminates the problem of data redundancy. Because material master records store data in a single database object, the same data can be shared by all departments, such as purchasing, inventory management, materials planning, and invoice verification.

6.   How is the information in material master records updated?

■ You can manually update the information in the material master records, however, there are some exceptions for which the information can be updated by the SAP R/3 system only, for example, administrative data.

7.   What are the types of industry sectors defined in the material master data?

■ The different types of industry sectors defined in the material master data are as follows:

☐ Aerospace and defense

☐ Beverage

☐ Chemical industry

☐ Food and related products

☐ Mechanical engineering

☐ Pharmaceuticals

☐ Plant engineering/construction

☐ Retail

☐ Retailing

☐ Service providers

8.   What data in the material master is maintained at the client level?

■ The general data, i.e., the data applicable to the company as a whole, is stored at the client level.

9.   What data in the material master is maintained at the company code level?

■ The data that is specific to a particular company and the plant and storage areas assigned to that company is maintained at the company code level.

10.   What are the plant-specific data in the material master?

■ The MRP data and forecast data are the plant-specific data in the material master.

11.   What is the lot size attribute of a material?

■ The lot size attribute represents the reorder quantity for a material. A material can have a periodic, optimum, or static (fixed) lot size.

12. How is material information structured in material master records?

■ Material information is structured in material master records on the basis of different criteria, such as the material's master detail (including its name, size, dimension, and weight), which shows its descriptive nature, and the material's detail related to control functions (such as material type, price control, and industry sector). Material master records also store information about the data that can be automatically updated by the system. For example, the stock level can be automatically updated by the system on the basis of the material data update.

13. What is a batch?

■ A batch is a group of materials combined into one quantity for various reasons. Very often, materials with the same characteristics and values are grouped into a batch. For example, in the chemical industry, a specified number of containers of a specific product may be considered a batch if they were produced at the same time and have the same physical and chemical characteristics.

14. Why is a batch record important?

■ A batch represents a quantity of a particular material processed at the same time with the same parameters. These materials, produced as one batch, have the same characteristics and values, which may vary from the materials of another batch produced on the same day.

■ A batch record is important because batch records indicate that the batch conforms to the current Good Manufacturing Procedures (GMP). The batch record also contains specific information about the product tested, analytical methods, and test results.

15. How do we create a batch?

■ You can create a batch record manually by using the transaction code MSC1N. The navigation path for creating a batch is: *SAP Menu > Logistics > Materials Management > Material Master > Batch > Create.*

16.   What are the important fields in a batch master record?

- The important fields in a batch master record are as follows:
    - □ *Production date*—Refers to the date when the batch was produced.
    - □ *Self-life expiration date*—Refers to the date when the life of the batch will expire.
    - □ *Available from*—Refers to the date from which the batch will be available to other departments.
    - □ *Batch status*—Allows the batch to be classified as having restricted or unrestricted use.
    - □ *Next inspection*—Refers to the next quality inspection date of the batch.
    - □ *Vendor batch*—Refers to the batch number assigned by the vendor.
    - □ *Class*—Allows the user to sort the batch for use in specific classes.
    - □ *Characteristics*—Helps in assigning a class to the batch.
    - □ *Release status*—Specifies the status of the batch.
    - □ *Linked document*—Helps the user to link the documents related to the batch.
    - □ *Document type*—Allows the user who is purchasing the batch to specify a document.
    - □ *Document*—Helps the user to select the relevant document.
    - □ *Document part*—Allows the user to enter the part of the document that is related to the batch.
    - □ *Version*—Specifies the document version of the batch.

17.   How can batch records be changed?

- You can change a batch record by using the transaction code MSC2N. The navigation path of changing the batch record is: *SAP Menu > Logistics > Materials Management > Material Master > Batch > Change.*

■ It is important to note that these changes to the batch record will also be available for review.

18. How do we delete a batch?

■ You can delete a batch by using the MSC2N transaction code. You can alternately delete a batch record by flagging the batch master record. For this, you need to first select the batch in the Change mode.

19. What is the Batch Information Cockpit?

■ The Batch Information Cockpit (BIC) is the main switching point, having a wide range of options for scrutiny and control of batches. It stores at a single location all the information related to the analysis of a particular batch.

20. What are the levels at which a batch number can be configured?

■ A batch number can be configured at several different levels: client level, plant level, and material level. You can select a batch number at any of the following levels:

□ *Client level*—When you configure a batch at the client level, you need to assign the batch number only once throughout the whole client. Only one batch number exists for each material assigned at this level.

□ *Plant level*—In SAP, the plant level is the default level for the batch number. At plant level, a batch number is unique for a plant and material. This means that you can have a batch of the same number at a different plant within the same company.

□ *Material level*—At this level, material numbers are assigned to the products. The material number helps to differentiate between two products in case their batch numbers are the same. The materials are identified by the combination of the material number and batch number.

21.   How are batch numbers assigned?

■ The batch number is predefined in SAP. You can change the batch numbers either by using the OMAD transaction code or by using the navigation path *IMG > Logistics-General > Batch Management > Batch Number Assignment > Maintain Internal Batch Number Assignment Range.*

Follow either of the two configuration steps to change the batch number:

☐ You can assign a batch number internally using the internal number range, either by using the OMCZ transaction code or by following the navigation path *Display IMG > Logistics-General > Batch Management > Batch Number Assignment > Activate Internal Batch Number Assignment > Activate Batch Number Assignment.*

☐ You can also configure the system to allow automatic numbering of a batch by following the navigation path *Display IMG > Logistics-General > Batch Management > Batch Number Assignment > Activate Internal Batch Number Assignment > Internal Batch Number Assignment for Assigned Goods Receipt.*

22.   What is a serial number?

■ A serial number is assigned to an item to identify it and to store information about it. A serial number is mostly used to refer to equipment such as motors, drills, or vacuums. In MM, an item of material contains a serial number as well as a material number. This combination helps to uniquely identify an item of material.

23.   What is a class type? How do we configure a class type?

■ A class type is the SAP system's top-level unit, which is used to control the SAP system's classes. It performs the following tasks:

☐ Defines the class objects

☐ Checks if class objects can be used in other classes or not

☐ Defines the class maintenance screen

■ You can configure a class type by using the following menu path: *SAP Customizing Implementation Guide > Cross Application Component > Classification System > Classes > Maintain Object Types and Material Types.*

24. How can we procure a master record for a material that does not have one?

■ There may be instances when a material does not have a master record. You can perform different functions in different situations to procure the master record. For example:

  ☐ You can create a material master record if there is no material master record for a particular material.

  ☐ You can extend the material master record if the material master record exists for a particular material but the user department does not have the master data.

  ☐ You can also extend the material master record if the material master record exists for a particular material and the user department has the master data but it has been entered in a different organizational level.

25. What is the importance of classification data?

■ Classification data allows you to search for materials on the basis of the characteristic values entered into the classes. This feature is very useful when the customer wants to search for a particular vendor and particular batches.

26. What is an ABC indicator?

■ An ABC indicator is an indicator assigned by the ABC analysis procedure. An ABC indicator provides details of the consumption value of the material involved in the ABC analysis. The ABC analysis is performed by multiplying the current price of the materials by their quantity. The different consumption values are given as follows:

  ☐ A materials—Important parts, high usage/consumption value

- □ B materials—Less important parts, medium usage/consumption value
- □ C materials—Relatively unimportant parts, low usage/consumption value

27.   What are the main master files used in MM?

- ■ The following are the main master files used in MM:
    - □ Material master file
    - □ Inventory master file
    - □ Vendor master file

28.   Give some examples of master data in MM.

- ■ Material master, material master general data (MARA), tax classification material (MLAN), info records, source list, and vendor master are examples of master data in MM.

29.   How do we create a vendor?

- ■ You can create a vendor by using the transaction code XK01 and performing the following steps:
    - □ Add the vendor name, company code, purchasing organization, account group, and vendor address.
    - □ Add the country, bank key, bank account, and the name of the account holder.
    - □ Save the data.
    - □ This creates a vendor record in the system.

30.   What is vendor master data?

- ■ Vendor master data contains details of each vendor that supplies materials or services to an enterprise. The vendor master data is stored in individual vendor master records consisting of data, such as the vendor's name, the vendor's address, the currency used for the transaction, payment terms, and the contact person's name (on the sales staff).

31.   What are the different sections in vendor master data?

- Following are the three sections in vendor master data:
  - *General data*—Provides general information about the vendor that can be entered into the system for creating vendor records. General data can provide the name, address, telephone, and fax of the vendor through specified search terms. Additional information can also be added to the vendor master record by the accounting and purchasing departments using the transaction code XK01.
  - *Accounting data*—Refers to financial information entered at the company code level. The financial information includes tax information, bank details, reconciliation account, payment terms, payment methods, and dunning information. You can enter this financial data using the transaction code FK01.
  - *Purchasing data*—Refers to data entered while creating a vendor at the purchasing organization level. Different purchasing organizations have different purchasing data. The purchasing data includes partner functions, purchasing default fields, and invoice verification indicators. You can enter this data using the transaction code MK01.

32.   What are the different fields in vendor master data?

- The different fields in vendor master data are as follows:
  - The name and address of the vendor
  - The currency in which the transaction will be done
  - The terms and conditions of payment
  - The names of important contact persons
  - The accounting information, such as the reconciliation account in the general ledger

33.   How do we create a vendor number range?

- When you create a number range, it is important to remember that vendor numbers, such as material numbers, can be assigned externally or internally. You can create vendor number ranges by selecting the following navigation path: *IMG > Financial Accounting > Vendor Accounts > Master Data > Preparations for Creating Vendor Master Data > Create Number Ranges for Vendor Accounts.*

■ For configuring the vendor number range, you should enter a unique number for the range, which is a two character field, and then specify the limit for the number range. The current number field is used to define the current number. The Ext. field specifies whether the number range is defined externally by the user.

34. What is dunning procedure? How can it be configured?

■ Sometimes, you may need to send a payment reminder or a dunning notice to a person or an organization to remind them of their outstanding debts. The process by which the system controls dunning is called dunning procedure. Dunning procedure can be configured by using the FBMP transaction code or the following navigation path: *IMG > Financial Accounting > Accounts Receivable and Accounts Payable > Business Transactions > Dunning > Dunning Procedure > Defining Dunning Procedures.*

35. How do we assign material to vendors?

■ Select the following navigation path to link vendors to materials: *SAP Menu > Logistics > Material Management > Purchasing > Master Data > Info Record > Create.* Alternatively, the ME11 transaction code is used for this purpose.

36. What is the transaction code to access the Materials Management Configuration menu?

■ The OLMS transaction code is used to access the Materials Management Configuration menu.

37. What are the various transaction codes to access the MM configuration?

■ The following are the various transaction codes to access the MM configuration:

Transaction Code	Description
OLMD	Accesses Material Management-Consumption Based Planning (MM-CBP)
OLMB	Accesses Material Management-Inventory Management (MM-IM)
OLME	Accesses Material Management-Purchase (MM-PUR)
OLML	Accesses Material Management-Warehouse Management
OLMS	Accesses the material master data
OLMW	Enables valuation and account assignment

38. Write the names of some important MM tables.

■ The following table lists the important MM table names:

Table Name	Purpose
EINA	Used for general data of the (purchasing) information record
MARC	Used in plant data for materials
EINE	Used for purchasing organization
MAST	Used for bills of material (BOM) link
MKPF	Used for header material document
MAKT	Used for material description
MARD	Used in storage location data for material
MARA	Used for general materials data
MBEW	Used for material valuation

39.   What are purchasing information records?

- Purchasing information records, also known as info records, contain information related to the material and the vendor who is supplying the material. They also contain details about the material, such as the current price.

40.   What are the categories of purchasing information records?

- The categories of purchasing information records are as follows:
  - □ *Standard*—Contains information for the standard purchase order. In this type of purchasing info record, you can create info records for materials and services that do not have master records.
  - □ *Subcontracting*—Contains ordering information for subcontract orders.
  - □ *Pipeline*—Contains information on commodities that are sent through a pipeline, such as oil or water.
  - □ *Consignment*—Contains information on materials that are in the vendor's possession and are kept by the vendor at some other premises at his own cost.

41.   What are the prerequisites for creating a purchasing info record?

- The prerequisites for creating a purchasing info record are as follows:
  - □ *Material number*—Before creating a purchasing info record, the material number of the material master record should be known.
  - □ *Manufacturer part number (MPN) material number*—Before ordering a material that has an MPN, you must know its MPN material number.
  - □ *Vendor number*—You should also know the number on the vendor master record.

- ☐ *Organizational level*—If the purchasing info record is for a particular purchasing organization or plant, then the code specific to that purchasing organization or plant is required.

42. How can we create a purchasing information record?

- ■ You can create a purchasing information record either manually or automatically by setting the Info Update indicator when maintaining a quotation, a purchase order, or an agreement.

43. Can a purchasing info record be created without a material number?

- ■ Yes, you can create a purchasing info record without a material number. If the material does not have a material number, you will need the following information to create the purchasing info record:
  - ☐ Material short text
  - ☐ Order unit
  - ☐ Material group
  - ☐ Short term key

44. How can we create an information record based on the material master?

- ■ First, you need to create the info record by selecting *SAP Menu > Master Data > Info Record > Create*. Enter details such as vendor number, material number, purchase organization, or plant number. Then enter the number of the information record (in case of external assignments). Next, enter the general data for vendors, ordered quantity, origin of data, supplying information, and customs tariff number. Then enter the planned delivery time, purchasing groups, and standard purchasing quantity. Check the control data and take the default value of tolerance data and the purchasing group from the material master record. Finally, enter the net price and then select *Go To > Texts* to display the text overview. If the PO text is already defined, it appears in the material master record; otherwise, it needs to be entered. After all these entries have been made, the record is saved.

45. What is the document management system (DMS) in SAP?

- The DMS in SAP helps you store external documents, such as pictures of the goods or material. By using the DMS, you can set the maximum size of the picture that can be uploaded in a document. The DMS helps to link these external documents with the appropriate SAP objects.

46. What is the document information record?

- The document information record is a master record containing information about the external documents, such as computer-aided design (CAD) drawings and material pictures. It also contains information about external documents, such as the external document's file name, file type, and location. Therefore, the document information record helps link the external documents with the SAP objects. The document information record stores the following information about the external documents:
  - □ *Document number*—Represents an alphanumeric number, which is used to identify the external document. This number can be a maximum of 25 characters.
  - □ *Document type*—Refers to the type of document. For example, the document type for CAD drawings is DRW. The document type can be a maximum of three characters.
  - □ *Document part*—Refers to a section of the document that is treated as a separate document.
  - □ *Document version*—Represents the document's version number.
  - □ *Document status*—Represents the document's status, such as in processing, locked, or rejected.

47.   How does one create a document?

■ You can create a document by using the CV01N transaction code or by using the following menu path: *SAP Menu > Logistics > Central Functions > Document Management System > Document > CVO1N-Create.*

48.   What are the key fields that one must specify when creating a document?

■ The key fields that you must specify while creating a document are:

☐ *Document number*—Refers to a unique alphanumeric number that is used to identify the document.

☐ *Document type*—Refers to a document type that categorizes a document.

☐ *Document part*—Refers to a section of a document that is treated as an individual document.

☐ *Document version*—Refers to a two-character number that represents the document version.

49.   How does one link a document to a material master record?

■ After creating a document, you can link it with the material master record by using the MM01 transaction code or by using the following menu path: *SAP Menu > Logistics > Materials Management > Material Master > Material > Create (General) > MM01- Immediately.*

50.   How do you link a document to a vendor master record?

■ Once you create a document, you can link that document with the vendor master record by using the XK01 transaction code or by using the following menu path: *SAP Menu > Logistics > Materials Management > Purchasing > Master Data > Vendor > Central > XK01- Create.*

51. How is the classification system used to describe a document?

- A DMS stores a large number of documents; it therefore can become quite difficult to find the right document. In such a case, the classification system uses a set of characteristics combined to form a class to describe a document. The class assigned to a document can be used to find a specific document in the DMS.

52. How can material numbers be assigned in a material master file?

- In the material master file, the material numbers are assigned at the configuration level. You can use either the OMSL transaction code or the following navigation path: *IMG > Logistics-General > Material Master > Basic Settings > Define Output Format for Material Numbers.*
- The configuration screen for defining the output format for a material number opens. In this screen, you need to enter the following data:
  - The length of the material number
  - The format of the material number
- There are two more fields in the screen which specify how the material number is stored. They are as follows:
  - Lexicographical indicator—Applies only for numeric material numbers.
  - Leading-zero indicator—Sets the material number with leading zeros.

If the lexicographical indicator is set, the system ignores the leading-zero indicator.

53. What data is contained in the information record?

- The information record contains data related to the units of measurement, such as the products, vendor price, materials used by specific vendors, and pricing conditions for a purchase organization. In addition, the tolerance limit of the

over/under delivery of data, planned delivery time, vendor
evaluation data, and availability status for goods are included
in the information record.

54. How do we change the standard price in the material master?

■ The standard price for the material data cannot be changed
  or updated directly. However, you can perform the following
  steps to change the standard price:

  ☐ Fill in the future fields price (MBEW-ZKPRS) and the
    effective date (MBEW-ZKDAT) for the materials.

  ☐ Select *Logistics > Materials Management > Valuation >
    Valuation Price Determination > Future Price > Activate.*

■ The standard price of the material master is changed.

55. What is the source of the "not allowed" error in the case of custom movement type creation?

■ You need to check the allowed transactions for the customized
  movement types and use the OMJJ transaction code.

56. Give the names of the tables where the header level and item data are stored in a purchase order.

■ The EKKO and EKPO are the two tables where the header and
  item level data are stored, respectively.

57. Give the names of the tables where the material master data is stored.

■ The MARA and MARC are the two tables where the material
  master data is stored.

58. What is the vendor evaluation? How is it maintained?

■ The vendor evaluation enables you to rate a vendor's performance by giving a score on a scale of 0 to 100. You can

also use transaction code ME61 and enter the purchase organization and vendor number to view the vendor's details.

59. List the components of the master data and their transaction codes.

■ The components of the master data and their transaction codes are as follows:

  ☐ Condition type—MEKA
  ☐ Vendor evaluation—ME61
  ☐ Vendor—MK01
  ☐ Quota arrangement—MEQ1
  ☐ Source list—ME01
  ☐ Info record—ME11

60. What is the name of the SAP program used to update or create material master records?

■ The RMDATIND program is used to update or create material master records.

61. What is storage location-specific material master data?

■ There may be a case when you need to store a material at more than one storage location. In that case, you need to create different material master records for each storage location in order to store the data. This is called storage location-specific material master data.

62. When is a production resource/tool (PRT) defined for a material?

■ If purchasing and inventory functions are carried out for a PRT, then a PRT is defined for a material.

63.   What transaction code is used to extend the material view?

- The MM50 transaction code is used to extend the material view.

64.   Give some examples of information related to a material's storage and warehousing.

- The following are some examples of information related to a material's storage and warehousing:
  - Volume
  - Unit of issue
  - Gross weight
  - Storage conditions
  - Hazardous materials number
  - Packaging dimensions

65.   What is a source list? What is the menu path to define a source list?

- A source list is used to identify sources of supply for certain materials. You can use the following menu path to define a source list: *Logistics > Materials Management > Purchasing > Source List*.

66.   How do we create a source list?

- You first need to enter the material number and plant data. Next, enter the source list records, validity period, time for procurement, vendor number, and purchasing organizations. Finally, enter the PPL (for procurement from outside), fixed source, and MRP control. The source list is then created. While entering the data, check whether the source data overlaps by selecting *List > Check Link*.

67.   What is the transaction code for creating a source list?

- The transaction code for creating a source list is ME01.

68. What transaction codes are used with a source list and what is their purpose?

■ Transaction codes used with a source list, along with their purpose, are given in the following table:

Transaction Code	Purpose
ME01	Maintains a source list
ME03	Displays a source list
ME04	Displays changes to a source list
ME05	Generates a source list
ME06	Analyzes a source list
ME07	Reorganizes a source list
ME0M	Displays a source list for material

69. What are material numbers in SAP?

■ Material numbers are unique numbers used to identify a material.

70. What does an industry sector control?

■ While creating the material master record for a material, you need to classify the material according to the industry type. This is called the industry sector. The industry sector controls the screen appearance, the screen sequence, and the appearance of industry-specific fields on individual screens in the material master record.

71. Can we change the industry sector of an existing material?

■ No, once assigned you cannot change the industry sector of an existing material.

72.   What is the material type of a material?

■ The material type represents a group of materials that have the same basic attributes. Various materials can be grouped under one material type on the basis of the following points:

   □ *Material purpose*—The purpose of the materials is the same. For example, configurable materials can have one material type and process materials can have a different material type.

   □ *Material number*—The pattern to assign numbers to the materials is the same. For example, all materials that are assigned numbers internally can be put in one material type, while the materials that are assigned number externally can have different material types.

   □ *Material number range*—All materials in a material type are grouped under the same material number range.

   □ *Material entry screen and sequence*—Details about the materials in a material type are managed by using the same material entry screen, and those screens have the same sequence number.

   □ *Material procurement*—The material procurement process is the same for all materials in a material type. For example, materials that are manufactured in-house have the same material type, while materials that are procured externally have different material types.

73.   What is a valuation category?

■ A valuation category is the standard used to distinguish the different partial stocks. In simple words, you can say that valuation category is the criteria that defines partial stocks. The standard system is comprised of a variety of valuation categories, such as B and H. B is used for a procurement type, in which the stock is divided up depending on whether it is procured externally or manufactured in-house. On the other hand, H is used for an origin type, in which the stock is divided on the basis of from where it was delivered. The valuation category in the material master record holds every material that has been assigned for valuation.

74.   What does the material type control?

■ The material type controls the material's stock management, which implies:

  ☐ If there is a change in the quantity of the material, it should be updated in the material master record.

  ☐ Along with changes in the material master record, there should also be changes in the stock accounts.

75.   What is the transaction code to create a material type?

■ MOS2 is the transaction code to create a material type.

76.   What are the general material types used in SAP?

■ The different general material types used in SAP are as follows:

  ☐ Additionals—VKHM

  ☐ Advertising media—WERB

  ☐ Apparel, seasonal—MODE

  ☐ Beverages—FGTR

  ☐ Competitor products

  ☐ Competitive products—WETT

  ☐ Configurable materials—KMAT

  ☐ Empties, industry—LEER

  ☐ Empties, retail—LGUT

  ☐ Equipment package

  ☐ Finished products—FERT

  ☐ Foods excluding perishables—FOOD

  ☐ Full products—VOLL

  ☐ Intra materials—INTR

  ☐ KANBAN containers—CONT

  ☐ Maintenance assemblies—IBAU

  ☐ Manufacturer parts—HERS

  ☐ Nonfoods—NOF1

  ☐ Nonstock materials—NLAG

  ☐ Nonvaluated materials—UNBW

  ☐ Operating supplies—HIBE

  ☐ Packaging materials—VERP

  ☐ Perishables—FRIP

  ☐ Pipeline materials—PIPE

  ☐ Process materials—PROC

  ☐ Product catalogs

  ☐ Product groups—PROD

  ☐ Production resources/tools—FHMI

  ☐ Raw materials—ROH

  ☐ Returnable packaging

  ☐ Semi-finished products—HALB

  ☐ Services—DIEN

  ☐ Spare parts—ERSA

  ☐ Trading goods—HAWA

  ☐ Value-only articles—WERT

  ☐ Waste

77. What material types are used while creating a new material?

■ Press the F4 key to select the material type for a material that you want to create. For example, the material type FHMI is used for PRT, the material type ROH is used for raw materials, and FERT is used for finished products.

78. What is the menu path to define material type attributes?

■ The menu path to define material type attributes is as follows: *Logistics Master Data: Material Master > Material > Control Data > Define Material Type Attributes.*

79.   Can we change the material type of a material?

■ Yes, you can change the material type of a material.

80.   What is the shelf life expiration date check? Where is it maintained?

■ The date up to which an organization can store and use the material is called the shelf life expiration date. The process to check the shelf life expiration date is called the shelf life expiration date check.

■ The shelf life expiration date check is maintained in the article master record or in the purchase order. You can allow the system to automatically manage the shelf life expiration date by activating the shelf life expiration date check while customizing for inventory management for the relevant site and movement type.

81.   How do we set user defaults for views?

■ You can set user defaults for views by selecting *Defaults > Views*.

82.   List the steps to create a profile.

■ You can create a profile by following these steps:
   □ Select *Profile > MRP Profile* from the Menu screen to display the *Initial Create Profile* screen.
   □ Enter the value in the key file that you want to assign in the profile.
   □ Select *Go To > Selection* to display the Selection screen.
   □ Enter a profile description and select the fields that you want to include in the profile.
   □ Select *Go To > Data* to display the Data screen.
   □ Enter your data in the Data screen and save the profile by selecting *Profile > Save*.

83. How do we change the characteristics?

■ The characteristics are the properties that describe the length, color, and other related features of an object. You can change the characteristics of an object by using the following menu path: *SAP Menu > Gross App. Components > Classification System > Master Data > Characteristics.*

Alternatively, the CT04 transaction code can be used to change the characteristics.

84. How do we create a class?

■ A class is a collection of a group of characteristics for a particular object. To create a class, you need to enter the class name and a description and then select the group. After saving the details, the class is created. Alternatively, you can use the CL01 transaction code for this purpose.

85. Can we include an ROH type in the sales view?

■ Usually, the ROH cannot be included in the sales view. However, the ROH can be included in the sales view when they are sold to procure finished products in return.

86. List the key fields of the m.5aterial master table.

■ The key fields of the material master table are material groups, material status, divisions, storage conditions, labs and offices, basic materials, container requirements, measure groups, container requirements, and temperature.

87. What are the major purchasing tables? List the transaction codes for them.

■ The major purchasing tables along with their transaction codes are as follows:

Purchasing Table	Transaction Code
Purchase requisition	EKBN
Purchase requisition account assignment	EBKN
Release documentation	EKAB
History of purchase documents	EKBE

88. What is nonvaluated material?

■ Material that is maintained on the basis of its quantity rather than its value is called nonvaluated material. Nonvaluated material can be withdrawn from stores or warehouses only when it is transferred to valuated stock.

89. What are the views in material master? Which data, in general, do these views contain?

■ The following are the views listed in material master:
  □ Basic Data 1 & 2
  □ Sales: Organization Data 1 & 2
  □ Sales: General/Plant Data
  □ Foreign Trade: Export Data
  □ Foreign Trade: Import Data
  □ Sales Text
  □ Purchasing
  □ Purchase Order Text
  □ MRP 1, 2, 3, 4
  □ Forecasting
  □ General Plant Data/Storage 1 & 2
  □ Warehouse Management 1 & 2
  □ Quality Management
  □ Accounting 1 & 2
■ In general, these views contain different types of data related to individual materials based on the view selected.

90. What are the fields in a material master file?

■ The fields in different views of a material master file are as follows:

☐ Basic Data 1
- Material description
- Basic unit of measure
- Material group
- Old material number
- X-plant material status–blocking option
- General item category
- Gross weight
- Net weight
- Volume

☐ Basic Data 2 – contains design drawing information

☐ Purchasing
- Basic unit of measure
- Purchasing group
- Material group
- Plant-specific material status–blocking option
- Source list
- Batch management–automatic PO
- Purchasing value key
- GR processing time (the number of days required after receiving a material for inspection; the material is later placed into the storage location)
- Critical part
- Manufacturer part number
- Manufacturer

☐ General Plant Data/Storage 1
- Basic unit of measure
- Temperature conditions
- Storage conditions
- Container requirements
- Hazards material number

- Batch management
- Shelf life expiration date (SLED)
□ General Plant Data/Storage 2
  - Plant
  - Gross weight
  - Net weight
  - Negative stock in plant
  - Profit center
□ Accounting 1
  - Basic unit of measure
  - Valuation class
  - Price control
  - Price unit
  - Valuation category
  - Currency
  - Moving and standard price
  - Total stock
  - Total value
  - Division
□ Accounting 2
  - Tax price 1, 2, 3
  - Commercial price 1, 2, 3
  - LIFO pool
□ Work Scheduling
  - Unit of issue
  - Production unit
  - Plant specific material status
  - Tolerance data
  - Material group
  - Batch management
  - Base quantity
□ Quality Management
  - Unit of issue
  - GR processing time

- Plant-specific material status
- Quality management (QM) control key
- QM procurement active

91. What are the important fields in the Basic Data view?

- The important fields in the Basic Data view are as follows:
  - □ Basic Data 1
    - Material description
    - Base unit of measure
    - Material group
    - Old material number
    - X-plant material status–blocking option
    - General item category
    - Authorization group
    - Gross weight
    - Net weight
    - Weight unit
    - Volume
    - Volume unit
    - Size/dimensions
    - EAN/UPC
  - □ Basic Data 2
    - Design drawing information
    - Environment (highly viscous/bulk/liquid)

92. How can we access the additional data screen?

- You can access the additional data screen in a material master record from any view by selecting additional data in the standard material master.

93.   What are the important fields in the Accounting view?

- The important fields in the Accounting view are as follows:
    - ☐ Accounting 1
        - Plant
        - Basic unit of measure
        - Valuation category
        - Valuation class
        - Price control
        - Price unit
        - Currency
        - Current period
        - Moving and standard price
        - Total stock
        - Total value
        - Division
        - Future price
        - Valid from
    - ☐ Accounting 2
        - Tax price 1, 2, 3
        - Commercial price 1, 2, 3
        - Devaluation indicator
        - Price unit
        - LIFO/FIFO relevance
        - LIFO pool

94.   What are the important fields in sales organization data?

- The different important fields in sales organization data are listed as follows:
    - ☐ General Data
        - Base unit of measure

- Division
- Sales unit
- Sales unit–not variable
- Unit of measure group
- X-distribution chain status
- DChain-specification status
- Delivering plant
- Material group
  □ Grouping Items
    - Material statistics group
    - Volume rebate group
    - General item category group
    - Pricing reference material
    - Product hierarchy
    - Commission group
    - Material pricing group
    - Account assignment group
    - Item category group
  □ Tax Data
    - Tax classification
  □ Quantity Stipulations
    - Minimum order quantity
    - Minimum delivery quantity
    - Delivery unit
    - Rounding profile
  □ Material Groups
  □ Product Attributes

95. What are the important fields in plant data?

- ■ The different important fields in plant data are listed as follows:
  □ General Data
    - Base unit of measure
    - Storage bin

- Temperature conditions
- Storage conditions
- Container requirements
- Hazardous material number
- Cycle counting–physical inventory indicator
- Cycle counting–fixed
- Number of goods receipt slips
- Label type
- Label form
□ Shelf-Life Data
- Maximum storage period
- Minimum remaining shelf life
- Period indicator for shelf-life expiration date (SLED)
- Storage percentage
- Time unit
- Total shelf life
- Rounding rule SLED
□ Weight Volume
- Gross weight
- Net weight
- Volume
- Size/dimensions
- Weight unit
- Volume unit
□ General Plant Parameters
- Profit center
- Distribution profile

96. What are the important fields in the Purchasing view?

- The important fields in the Purchasing view are as follows:
  □ Base unit of measure
  □ Order unit

- Purchasing group
- Material group
- Plant-specific material status–blocking option
- Valid from
- Tax indicator for material
- Source list
- Batch management–automatic PO
- Purchasing value key
- GR processing time
- Just-in-time (JIT) scheduled indicator
- Critical part
- Manufacturer part number
- Manufacturer

97.   How can we create a material in SAP?

- Perform the following steps to create a material in SAP:
  - Select *Logistics > Materials Management > Material Master* to open the Material Master menu.
  - In the Material Master menu, select either *Material > Create (General) or Material > Create (Special)*.
  - After selecting the Create (General) option, double-click one of the following options to open the initial screen for creating a material master record:
    - MM01–Immediately (if the data needs to be available immediately) opens the initial screen of Create Material.
    - MM11–Schedule (if the material master record needs to be scheduled) opens the initial screen of Schedule Creation of Material.
  - After selecting the Create (Special) option, double-click the Material Type option (if a material master record of a particular material type needs to be created) to open the initial screen to create a material master record. In this case, you do not need to enter the material type on the

following screen. However, scheduling cannot be done for material master records of this type.

☐ In the initial screen, enter the following data:

- Material number (only when assigning an external number and if allowed by the material type; otherwise, this field remains blank).

- Industry sector

- Material type (not required if you have created the material by selecting *Material > Create (Special) > Material Type*).

☐ In case you want to refer to another material master record, enter the reference material number under the Copy From option.

☐ Enter the following data to schedule the material master record:

- Key date

- Change number

■ If a key date is entered, the system checks to ensure that it does not precede the valid from date of the change number. If a key date is not specified, the valid from date of the change number is used. Note that in both the cases the date must be in the future.

☐ Press the Enter key. The Select View(s) dialog box appears.

☐ Now, select the views for which you want to enter data.

☐ Press the Enter key. The Organizational Levels dialog box appears.

☐ Set the organizational levels as needed and, if appropriate, enter a profile.

☐ If you provide a reference material, then you will need to provide the organizational levels of the reference material, whose data needs to be copied as default values, under the Copy From option; otherwise, the system will copy only the data at the client level.

☐ Press the Enter key. The first user department data screen appears.

☐ If the data is not already copied from the reference material, specify the description of material and the unit of measure in the respective fields. This information is compulsory and is similar for all user departments. Enter the data here after consulting with other users.

☐ Specify the data for your user department as needed.

☐ Press the Enter key. The data screen for the next user department appears.

☐ Enter the data for the other departments selected in the Select View(s) dialog box. A message will appear to inform you when you have reached the data screen for the last user department selected.

■ Suppose you want to enter data for a user department that you did not select in the Select View(s) dialog box. You can access the user department directly by selecting it, but only if you have the proper rights to process data for this user department and the user department is allowed by the material type.

☐ Save the data entered. Finally, the initial screen appears where you can start to create the next material master record.

98. What does "extending a material" mean? How is this done?

■ If a user department has already stored data on a material in the material master record and you want to enter data for the same material in another user department, you are not required to create another material master record. Rather, you can extend the material so that the data that is appropriate to your own user department can be included. The steps to extend a material in SAP are as follows:

☐ Select *Logistics > Materials Management > Material Master* to open the Material Master menu.

☐ In the Material Master menu, select *Material > Create (General)*.

☐ Double-click one of the following options to open the initial screen for creating a material master record:

- MM01–Immediately (if the data needs to be available immediately) opens the initial screen of Create Material.

- MM11–Schedule (if the material master record needs to be scheduled) opens the initial screen of Schedule Creation of Material.

☐ In the initial screen, enter the material number in the material field.

☐ You are not required to enter any industry sector or material types, as the system copies them from the existing material master record.

☐ Enter the following data to schedule the material master record in the initial screen of Schedule Creation of Material:

- Key date
- Change number

■ If a key date is entered, the system checks to ensure that it does not precede the valid from date of the change number. If a key date is not entered, the valid from date of the change number is used. Note that in both the cases the date must be in the future.

☐ Press the Enter key.

■ On the initial screen, if the data entered for the industry sector and material type varies from the data already entered by a different department, then the data is replaced by the value in the existing material master record and a warning is issued that is confirmed by pressing the Enter key. The Select View(s) dialog box appears.

☐ Now, select the views for which you want to enter data.

☐ Press the Enter key. The Organizational Levels dialog box appears.

☐ Set the organizational levels as needed and, if appropriate, enter a profile.

☐ Press the Enter key. The first user department data screen appears and a message will appear to inform you that you are extending the material master record.

- The data already entered and the data that is valid for all user departments are displayed.
  - □ Specify your data as needed and save it. Finally, the initial screen appears where you can continue extending material.

99. How can we create a material master record?

- Perform the following steps to create a material master record:
  - □ Log on to the SAP system.
  - □ Enter transaction code MM01.
  - □ Select retail (for example) from the industry sector drop-down list and leave the material text box blank. The system automatically assigns a material number.
  - □ Click the Enter button (✅) on the toolbar. This opens the Select View(s) dialog box.
  - □ Select the Basic Data 1, Sales: Sales Organization, Sales: General/Plant Data, Sales Text, and Accounting 1 views in the dialog box.
  - □ Click the Continue (Enter) button in the Select View(s) dialog box. This opens the Organizational Levels dialog box.
  - □ In the Organizational Levels dialog box, enter the following data:

Field	Data
Plant	2300
Sales Org.	2300
Distr. Channel	10

NOTE: The data entered for all the fields in this chapter are dummy data. These may vary according to different organizations.

  - □ Click the Continue (Enter) button. This opens the Create Finished Product page.

☐ On the Basic Data 1 tab page, enter the following data:

Field	Data
Material	Shirt
Base Unit of Measure	PC
Material Group	02004
Division	09
Gross Weight	0.3
Net Weight	0.3
Weight Unit	KG

☐ Click the Enter button on the toolbar. This displays the Sales: Sales Organization tab page.

☐ On this page, enter the following data:

Field	Data
Tax Classification	0

☐ Click the Enter button on the toolbar. This opens the Sales: General/Plant tab page.

☐ On this page, enter the following data:

Field	Data
Availability Check	01
Trans. Grp	0001
Loading Grp	0001

☐ Click the Enter button on the toolbar. This opens the Sales Text tab page.

☐ On this page, enter the following data:

Field	Data
Language	English
Material	Shirt

☐ Click the Enter button on the toolbar. This opens the Accounting 1 tab page.

☐ On this page, enter the following data:

Field	Data
Valuation Class	7925
Standard Price	50

☐ Click the Save button on the toolbar and note the material number generated by the system.

☐ Keep clicking the Exit button on the toolbar until you return to the SAP Easy Access page.

100. How can we change a material master record?

■ You can perform the following steps to change a material master record:

☐ Log on to the SAP system.

☐ Select *Logistics > Materials Management > Material Master > Material > Change > MM02–Immediately* to start the transaction. This opens the Change Material (Initial Screen) page.

☐ Enter the material number for which you want to change the master record.

☐ Click the Enter button on the toolbar. This opens the Select View(s) dialog box.

☐ Click the Select button to select all the views in the dialog box.

☐ Click the Continue (Enter) button in the dialog box. This opens the Organizational Levels dialog box.

☐ Enter the plant number in the Organizational Levels dialog box.

☐ Click the Continue (Enter) button. This opens the Change Material XXXX (Finished Product) page, where XXXX is the material number.

☐ Select the Basic Data 1 tab and make the appropriate changes in the fields to change the basic data information.

☐ Select the Accounting 1 tab and make the appropriate changes to change the accounting data information.

☐ Select the Sales Text tab and make the appropriate changes to change the sales text information.

☐ After making all the changes, click the Save button on the toolbar.

☐ Click the Exit button on the toolbar until you return to the SAP Easy Access page.

101. List the steps to delete a material master record.

■ Perform the following steps to delete a material master record:

☐ Log on to the SAP system.

☐ Select *Logistics > Materials Management > Material Master > Material > Flag for Deletion > MM06–Immediately* to start the transaction. This opens the Flag Material for *Deletion: Initial Screen* page.

☐ Enter the material number that you want to delete in the material text box.

☐ Enter the plant number in the plant text box.

☐ If required, enter the storage location in the storage location text box.

■ Leave the change number text box blank. The system automatically assigns an internal change number.

☐ Click the Enter button on the toolbar. This opens the *Flag Material for Deletion: Data Screen* page.

☐ Select the material check box to set all the data that is flagged for deletion.

☐ Select the check box associated with the plant number to delete the material for a specific plant.

- ☐ Select the check box associated with the storage location number to delete the stock material for a specific storage location only.

- ☐ Click the Save button to save the settings. When the archive and delete programs run again, the system processes only those materials that are flagged for deletion.

- ☐ Click the Exit button on the toolbar until you return to the SAP Easy Access page.

102. How can we display the material master record on the SAP system?

- ■ Perform the following steps to display a material master on the SAP system:

  - ☐ Log on to the SAP system.

  - ☐ Select *Logistics > Materials Management > Material Master > Material > Display > MM03–Display Current* to start the transaction. This opens the *Display Material (Initial Screen)* page.

  - ☐ Enter the material number in the material text box.

  - ☐ Click the Enter button on the toolbar. This opens the *Select View(s)* dialog box.

  - ☐ Select the view(s) whose material data you want to display.

  - ☐ Click the Continue (Enter) button in the *Select View(s)* dialog box. This opens the *Organizational Levels* dialog box.

  - ☐ Enter the organizational levels fields, such as plant, sales organization, and distribution channel.

  - ☐ Click the Continue (Enter) button. This opens the *Display Material XXXX* (Finished Product) page with all the selected views.

  - ☐ Select a particular tab to access the data on the tab page.

  - ☐ Click the Exit button on the toolbar until you return to the SAP Easy Access page.

■ For updating information, the MM02 transaction code may be used for the particular material number.

103. How do we move a material master record from one SAP system to another?

■ You can use one of two ways to move data from one SAP system to another.
   □ Direct input
   □ Application link enabling (ALE)

104. What is the transaction code to display material in SAP MM?

■ MM03 is the transaction code to display material in SAP MM.

105. What is the purchasing value key?

■ It is the key that determines the following:
   □ Reminder keys—keys that help determine the number of days before or after the vendor must be reminded about material procurement
   □ Under delivery tolerance limit and over delivery tolerance limit
   □ Order acknowledgement requirements in a purchase order

106. How can we configure the purchasing value key?

■ You can configure the purchasing value key by performing the following steps:
   □ Open the SAP Implementation Guide.
   □ Select *Materials Management > Purchasing > Material Master > Define Purchasing Value Keys*. This opens the

change view *Default Values: Material Master: Overview* page.

- ☐ Click the New Entries button. This opens the *New Entries: Details of Added Entries* page.
- ☐ Enter the appropriate values in the fields.
- ☐ Click the Save button on the toolbar.

107. Define "material group."

- ■ A material group is a classification or grouping of materials and services by their characteristics.

108. Define "material status."

- ■ The material status is an indicator maintained in the material master record to restrict the use of a material. You can restrict the use of a material for specific functions by assigning a value to material status.

109. What is the base unit of measure of a material? What are the other units of measure used in SAP for a material?

- ■ The base unit of measure of a material is the unit used to manage the stock of a material. In inventory management, the base unit is the same as the stock-keeping unit.
- ■ Different departments have their own material measurement units. The material measurement units, except the base unit, are called alternative material measurement units. The alternative material measurement units are as follows:
  - ☐ Order unit
  - ☐ Sales unit
  - ☐ Unit of issue
  - ☐ Warehouse management (WM) unit

110. How do we create a vendor master record?

■ You can create a vendor master record by using the following steps:

□ Select *Logistics > Materials Management > Purchasing > Master Data > Vendor > Central > XK01 - Create* to start the transaction. This opens the *Create Vendor: Initial Screen* page.

□ On this page, enter the following data:

Field	Data
Vendor	Any number from 1000 to 1999
Company Code	1000
Purchasing Organization	1000
Account Group	LIEF
Reference Vendor	1080
Reference Company Code	1000
Reference Purchasing Organization	1000

□ Click the Enter button on the toolbar. This opens the *Create Vendor: Address* page.

□ On this page, enter the following data:

Field	Data
Title	Company, Dr., Mr., or Ms.
Name	Any
Search Term 1/2	Any
Street/House Number	Any
Postal Code/City	Any 5-digit numerical value
Country	DE
Language	German

☐ Click the Enter button on the toolbar until the *Create Vendor: Accounting Information Accounting* page appears.

☐ Ensure that 161000 appears in the *Recon. Account* text box.

☐ Click the Enter button on the toolbar until the *Create Vendor: Purchasing Data* page appears.

☐ Ensure that the order currency is EUR.

☐ Click the Enter button on the toolbar until the *Create Vendor: Partner Functions* page appears.

☐ Click the Save button on the toolbar to complete the creation of the vendor master record.

☐ Click the Exit button until you return to the SAP Easy Access page.

111. How can we change a vendor master record?

■ You can perform the following steps to change a vendor master record:

☐ Select *Logistics > Materials Management > Purchasing > Master Data > Vendor > Central > XK02 - Change* to start the transaction. This opens the *Change Vendor: Initial Screen* page.

☐ Enter the vendor account number in the vendor text box, the company code in the company code text box, and the purchasing organization in the purchasing organization text box.

☐ Select the check boxes associated with the screen names under general data, company code data, and purchasing organization data to specify which screens you want to display.

☐ Click the Enter button on the toolbar. This opens the *Change Vendor: XXXX* page where XXXX specifies the screen selected on the initial screen page to display.

☐ Make the required changes to the appropriate fields.

☐ Click the Enter button on the toolbar to open the next page.

☐ Make the changes to the appropriate fields.

- ☐ Click the Enter button on the toolbar to open the next page to make the appropriate changes. Repeat this step until the appropriate changes are made on all the pages.

- ☐ Click the Enter button on the toolbar. This opens the Last Data Screen Reached dialog box, which asks whether to save the changes.

- ☐ Click the Yes button to save the changes. After saving the changes, you will come back to the Change Vendor: Initial Screen page.

- ☐ Click the Exit button until you return to the SAP Easy Access page.

112. How can we block a vendor?

- ■ You can perform the following steps to block a vendor:

  - ☐ Select *Logistics* > *Materials Management* > *Purchasing* > *Master Data* > *Vendor* > *Central* > *XK05 - Block* to start the transaction. This opens the *Block/Unblock Vendor: Initial Screen* page.

  - ☐ Enter the vendor account number in the vendor text box, the company code in the company code text box, and the purchasing organization in the purchasing organization text box.

  - ☐ Click the Enter button on the toolbar. This opens the *Block/ Unblock Vendor: Details* page.

  - ☐ Select all company codes or selected company code check boxes to block posting from all company codes or a specific company code.

  - ☐ Select all purchasing organizations or selected purchasing organization check boxes to block purchasing from all purchasing organizations or a specific purchasing organization.

  - ☐ Click within the block function text box and then click the button next to it to specify the block function. This opens the *Functions That Will Be Blocked* dialog box.

  - ☐ In the dialog box, select a block function from the list and click the Copy button. This closes the *Functions That Will Be Blocked* dialog box and sets the block function number in the block function text box.

     ☐ Click the Save button on the toolbar to save the changes and to return back to the *Block/Unblock Vendor: Initial Screen* page.

113. What is the vendor subrange?

■ The vendor subrange is defined as a subdivision of the total range of products provided by a vendor. Vendor subranges are required when you create or maintain material master data.

114. What is a one-time vendor?

■ A one-time vendor is a vendor who rarely or only once supplies materials or articles to your company. For such vendors, you do not need to create a separate master record because the master records have no use after the business transaction is completed. Therefore, you can collectively create a master record for all one-time vendors.

CHAPTER 4
PROCUREMENT AND PURCHASING

Procurement and Purchasing

1. What are the special stocks used in materials management (MM)?

- Special stocks are stocks that are managed separately regardless of whether they belong to your company. The company manages a material by using a data record, which contains all the required information. The different types of special stocks are as follows:
  - Sales order stock
  - Returnable packaging with customer
  - Consignment stock at customer
  - Vendor consignment stock
  - Returnable transport packaging
  - Subcontracting
  - Pipeline

2. What are the differences between company-owned special stocks and externally-owned special stocks?

- The differences between company-owned special stocks and externally-owned special stocks are listed in the following table:

Company-Owned Special Stocks	Externally-Owned Special Stocks
Stocks that belong to the company but are stored with the wholesaler or the customer are called company-owned special stocks.	Stocks that belong to the wholesaler or the customer but are stored at the company are called externally-owned special stocks.
Company-owned special stocks are managed at the production level.	Externally-owned special stocks are managed at the place where they are stored.

3. Why do organizations need negative stock?

- Organizations need negative stock when a material is shipped to a customer and production is not confirmed or there is not enough stock to satisfy the requirement. The system still allows the issuing of the material, and inventory shows a negative quantity of stock until the production of the material is confirmed.

4. What are special procurement types?

- In a normal purchasing system, the customer purchases the goods from the wholesaler/retailer and the possession of the goods transfers from the wholesaler/retailer to the customer. This might not be the case with special procurement types, where the transfer of goods may not necessarily be from the wholesaler/retailer to the customer directly. For example, you might order a good for a friend of yours, who, in turn, purchases the good from the wholesaler/retailer and then transfers the good to you. The friend is the third party involved in this process. Therefore, the possession of the good indirectly transfers to the customer. This type of procurement is called the special procurement type. The special procurement type defines the external procurement or in-house production of the material. The following list shows the special procurement types available in the SAP system:

☐ Consignment

☐ Subcontracting

☐ Stock transfer using the stock transport order (STO)

☐ Production in another plant

☐ Third-party processing

☐ Returnable transport packaging

☐ Pipeline handling

5.   Define "consignment stock." What are the main features of consignment stock?

■ Consignment, in a general sense, is the act of holding the ownership of materials but storing the materials at some other premises until the materials are sold or shifted somewhere else. The stored materials are known as consignment stock in the SAP system. Therefore, stock that is stored at the customer's premises but is the supplier's property until the stock is transferred to the customer's stock list is called the consignment stock. The main features of the consignment stock are as follows:

☐ You can combine the consignment stock with your available stock at any point in time.

☐ You can evaluate the consignment stock in any currency.

☐ The price of the consignment stock fluctuates. This means that you can determine the price of the consignment according to the market conditions.

☐ You can price the consignment stock in any unit.

☐ You can use different features of purchasing, such as discounts, in the consignment stock.

☐ The consignment stock is evaluated at a price quoted by different vendors.

6.   How is the pricing of consignment stocks done? What information does the consignment information record contain?

- Prior to ordering a material from a vendor or posting a goods receipt to the consignment stock, you need to obtain the consignment price. If the consignment material is ordered from several vendors, the system maintains the consignment stock of each vendor separately. The reason the system maintains the consignment stock separately is that the price of the consignment stock may vary from one vendor to another.

- The consignment information (info) record contains the consignment price required for the purpose of material valuation and accounting.

7.   How are consignment stocks created?

- Consignment stocks are created in the normal purchase order (PO) or requisition, but the main thing to consider is that you must enter the K category for the consignment item. As a result, the goods issued are posted to consignment stores and the invoice receipt is not generated.

8.   Define "consignment cycle."

- Consignment cycle is similar to the purchase cycle, except that when you create goods receipts of the consignment stocks, only quantity (QTY) is updated and no accounting documents are created. Once the goods are utilized, consignment is settled. The value of the consumed or issued consignment stocks is taken from the active purchase info record.

9.   How is consignment material procured?

- Consignment material is procured through purchase requisitions, POs, and outline agreements.

10.   How can we see the consignment stocks in SAP?

- You can see the consignment stocks in SAP by using the following functions:
  - ☐ Display consignment info record
  - ☐ Display the stock overview
  - ☐ Display consignment stocks

11.   How can we take consignment stocks into our own stock?

- You can take consignment stocks from the vendor into your own stock by performing the following steps:
  - ☐ Select *Goods Movement > Transfer Posting* to display the initial screen.
  - ☐ Enter the plant name and the location where you want to store the materials.
  - ☐ Select *Movement Type > Transfer Posting > Consignment > Consignment to Own*.
  - ☐ Select Continue to display the collective entry screen.
  - ☐ Enter the name of the vendor, the materials, and the quantity of materials.
  - ☐ Enter the receiving storage location if you want to store the materials in another storage location.
  - ☐ Post the document. This makes the vendor liable to change the storage location of the materials.

12.   Can we do the physical inventory check of consignment stocks?

- Yes, you can do the physical inventory check of consignment stocks. To do the physical inventory check, perform the following operations:
  - ☐ Create a physical inventory document
  - ☐ Enter the physical inventory count
  - ☐ Post the inventory differences

13. How can we invoice in the case of consignment stocks?

■ You can invoice in the case of consignment stocks by performing either of the following:
  □ Invoice with PO
  □ Invoice without PO

14. What is subcontracting?

■ Subcontracting can be defined as the processing of materials by an external supplier.

15. How is subcontracting used in MM?

■ Subcontracting is the process by which the vendor receives the materials to produce the end product. Subcontracting involves the following procedures:
  □ You order the end product by using the subcontract order. The components that the vendor needs to manufacture the end product are mentioned in the PO.
  □ During the inventory management process, the components are posted to the stock of material provided to the vendor. Later, the components are supplied to the vendor.
  □ The vendor then processes the service and delivers the materials ordered. The consumption of the components is posted.
  □ If, after posting the goods receipt, the vendor notifies you that the quantity of the components actually consumed is different than planned in the PO, you must make an adjustment.
  □ The vendor then charges for the service, for which the invoice is posted in Invoice Verification.

16. What information does the subcontracting info record contain?

■ A subcontracting info record consists of ordering information related to subcontract orders. For example, if you entered into a contract with an outside source for the assembly of a component, the subcontracting info record would contain the price specified by the vendor for the assembly work.

17.   How do we create a subcontracting purchase order (PO)?

■ Perform the following steps to create a subcontracting PO:

☐ Enter the material to order and the category of the item for subcontracting (L) in the order item.

☐ Press the Enter key to display the screen for component processing.

☐ In the component processing screen, enter the components required by the vendor to manufacture the ordered material (end product). When entering the components, you need to take care of the following points:

☐ You do not need to enter the date required for the components. The system proposes this date when you press the Enter key. It is calculated as follows:

■ Delivery date of the item (planned delivery time)

☐ If you do not wish the quantity of the components to be altered, even if the order quantity of the end product is changed, then set the indicated field to fixed quantity.

☐ If you want to allocate a particular batch of the component to the vendor for the manufacture of the ordered material, enter the desired batch.

☐ To determine whether or not the components are available on the date required, select *Component List > Component Availability*.

☐ When you enter a bill of material as the material in the subcontract order, the components are automatically created.

☐ You can also determine the components in the bill of material at a later date (for example, if the bill of material is subsequently changed) by selecting *Item > Go to > Components > New BOM Explosion*. The existing entry of the components is removed and again determined in the bill of material.

☐ Save the PO.

■ When you print the PO, the components are printed per order item.

18.   How can we view the stocks provided to a vendor?

- The stocks of material provided to a vendor can be viewed by using the SC Stock Monitoring for Vendor report. The report can be accessed by selecting *Purchase Order > Reporting > SC Stocks per Vendor* from the menu. With this report, the current status of the stocks, planned issues, and planned receipts can be viewed.

19.   How are components (materials) provided to the vendor?

- The components, or rather the quantities of the components required to manufacture the end product, are provided in the stock of material to be provided to the vendor. The stock of material provided to the vendor is the total valuated stock that is available for MRP. The total valuated stock is managed at the plant level, at the site of the vendor. This stock can be either an unrestricted-use or quality-inspection stock. The unrestricted-use stock refers to the valuated stock of a material that is owned by the company and does not have any restrictions on its usage. The quality-inspection stock is intended to be used only for quality inspection. The components can be provided to a vendor in the following ways:
    - ☐ Posting the components from the unrestricted-use stock
    - ☐ Receiving the components from another vendor

20.   How are components consumed in subcontracting?

- In subcontracting, the end product is ordered by using a subcontract order. The materials or components required by the vendor to manufacture the end product are mentioned in the PO. The components are posted to the stock of the material provided to the vendor during inventory management. When the components are supplied to the vendor, the vendor manufactures the end product and delivers it. At this point, the goods receipt is posted with a reference to the subcontract order. The goods receipt also contains the posting of the consumption of the components from the stock of material provided to the vendor. If the components consumed by the vendor are more or less than that specified in the PO, an adjustment needs to be posted to correct the consumption of components.

21. Why do we need to create physical inventory documents for an inventory cycle-count procedure of a material or materials?

■ For a cycle-count procedure, the physical inventory documents are needed because these are used to record inventory levels of the materials.

22. What is the difference between planned and unplanned consumption?

■ The difference between planned consumption and unplanned consumption is that planned consumption is updated if goods are withdrawn from stock with a reservation, whereas unplanned consumption is updated if goods are withdrawn from stock without a reservation.

23. How can we provide components to the vendor or subcontractor with and without a PO reference?

■ You can provide components to a vendor or subcontractor with and without a PO reference when the components are posted from the unrestricted-use stock to the stock of material provided to the vendor. To post components without a PO reference, perform the following steps:

☐ Select *Goods Movement > Transfer Posting* from the Inventory Management menu.

☐ Enter the issuing plant and storage location.

☐ Select *Movement Type > Transfer Posting > Stock with Subcontractor > From Unrestricted.*

☐ Press the Enter key. The collective entry screen appears.

☐ Enter the vendor and the individual components.

☐ Post the document. As a result, the unrestricted-use stock at the issuing storage location decreases and the stock of material provided to the vendor at the vendor's site increases.

- Components can also be provided with a PO reference, that is, for existing POs, in any of the following ways:
  - As a goods issue from the *SC Stock Monitoring for Vendor* menu
  - As a delivery through shipping from the *SC Stock Monitoring for Vendor* menu
  - By using the *Inventory Management* menu

24. How can one vendor obtain components from another vendor or third party?

- The components can be provided by a third party, such as another vendor. In this case, the subcontractor is specified as the delivery address in the PO. This implies that the components are delivered directly to the subcontractor. To order components for a subcontract order from another vendor, perform the following steps:
  - Select *Purchase Order > Create > Vendor Known from the Purchasing* menu.
  - Enter the vendor of the components and the desired plant.
  - Enter the components.
  - Select *Item > More Functions > Delivery Address*. A dialog box appears in which the delivery address can be entered.
  - Enter the number of the subcontractor in the vendor field.
  - Select the SC vendor box. The components at the goods receipt are posted to the stock of material provided to the vendor.
  - Save the PO.

25. How do we verify invoices for subcontracting POs?

- We verify invoices for subcontracting POs in the same way as we do for regular POs.

26. How do we attach a document to the PO?

■ A document can be manually attached to a PO by using the document management system in SAP. In cases where the PO is prepared using transaction code ME21N, no attachment can be added. You need to save the PO and reopen it with the transaction code ME22N. Click the Service for Object button, select *Service Object Button > Create > Create Attachment*, and then select the file to be attached.

27. How do we know if the PO has been issued?

■ You first need to open the requisition screen by performing the following steps: Select *Materials Management > Purchasing > Purchase Requisition > Display*. The next step is to select an item in the selection box and then click the general characteristics icon. The screen appears in which you select the "order statistics in the purchase order" field. If there is no number, then the PO has not been issued.

28. How can we create a subcontract order?

■ You can create a subcontract order by performing the following steps:
   ☐ Enter the end product to be ordered and the item category for subcontracting (L) in the order item.
   ☐ Press the Enter key to display the screen for component processing.
   ☐ Enter the components required by the vendor to manufacture the end product.
   ☐ Save the PO.

29. What is STO? What are its advantages?

■ STO is the acronym for stock transport order. It can be defined as a PO used to transport material from one plant to another within the same corporate enterprise. For example, you would use the STO for transferring materials between two plants or between the enterprise and a third-party contractor.

With the help of the STO, the cost incurred due to the delivery of the transfer materials is added to the transferred materials. The advantages of transferring materials with an STO are as follows:

☐ A goods receipt can be generated at the receiving plant.

☐ A transport vendor and delivery costs can be specified in the STO.

☐ The purchase requisitions created in the MRP can be changed to an STO, because the STO is part of the MRP.

☐ The goods issued can be specified by using a delivery through Shipping (LE-SHP) or Inventory Management (MM-IM).

☐ The goods receipt can be posted directly to consumption.

☐ The PO history can be used to monitor the entire process of stock transfer.

30. Is the goods receipt/invoice receipt (GR/IR) account needed in inventory?

■ When you are involved with inventory, then the system needs a GR/IR account. When you are not involved with inventory, then the system does not need a GR/IR account. In such a case, the system needs a GR account only, instead of a GR/IR account.

31. How is stock transfer done between the plants? What are one-step and two-step stock transfer?

■ Stock transfer between different plants is performed in Inventory Management. A stock transfer can happen between plants with the same or different company codes. In a stock transfer between plants, the sales department in the issuing plant and the purchasing department in the receiving plant are involved. The stock transfer between plants can be performed in a one-step or two-step procedure.

☐ *One-step stock transfer*—Refers to the procedure in which the quantity of stock issued from the issuing plant is the same as the quantity of stock received at the receiving plant. In this type of stock transfer, the entry for posting the transfer of stock is made in Inventory Management. The transfer posting can then be planned with or without a reservation and valuated in the issuing plant. In the case of plants having different company codes, two accounting documents are created for transfer posting. The quantity of the transferred stock is posted from the unrestricted-use stock of the issuing plant to the unrestricted-use stock of the receiving plant. The unrestricted-use stock in the issuing plant therefore decreases by the amount of the transferred stock and the unrestricted-use stock in the receiving plant increases by the amount of the transferred stock.

☐ *Two-step stock transfer*—Refers to the procedure in which the stock remains in transit until it is received at the receiving plant. In a two-step stock transfer, the decrease in stock in the issuing plant is posted first. The quantity of the transferred stock is then managed in the stock in transfer in the receiving plant. When the placement is posted in the receiving plant, the transferred stock becomes part of the unrestricted-use stock in the receiving plant. In a two-step stock transfer, the transfer posting cannot be planned by creating a reservation. Similar to the one-step stock transfer, two accounting documents are created for the transfer posting in case there are plants that have different company codes.

32. Define "lot size."

■ The lot size is the quantity of materials used for reordering. It can be static, periodic, optimum, or fixed in attributes.

33. What is a reservation?

■ A reservation is a document that ensures the availability of materials in the warehouse when materials are required for transfer to a customer. It contains information, such as which materials are needed, what quantities of materials are required, and when or where the materials are needed. It helps the MRP system to avoid lack of stock in the warehouse.

34.   What transaction codes are used with reservations?

- The following transaction codes are used with reservations:
  - MB21—Creates a reservation
  - MB22—Changes a reservation
  - MB23—Displays a reservation
  - MB25—Displays lists of reservations

35.   How is the list of all reservations in the systems displayed?

- The reservation list is displayed by running the RM07RESL report.

36.   What is the difference between stock transfer and transfer posting?

- Stock transfer is the physical movement of goods from one store to another store or one plant to another plant. Transfer posting is the movement of goods from one stock type to another or from one storage location to another storage location within a plant.

37.   What is the transaction code to create movement types?

- OMJJ is the transaction code to create movement types.

38.   How can we create movement types?

- Perform the following steps to create movement types:
  - Select the standard movement type 201 from the *Determine Work Area Entry* dialog box.
  - Click the copy icon and then overwrite 201 with Z01.
  - Select the new movement type Z01 from the *Determine Work Area Entry* dialog box.
  - Select *Reversal > Follow-On Movement*.
  - Enter the reversal movement type.

39. Why is the stock transfer order set up in the initial configuration?

■ The stock transfer order is created in case there is interplant stock transfer through the SD module.

40. How is stock transferred with and without delivery?

■ A stock transfer can be made with or without delivery. In a stock transfer without delivery, inventory management as well as purchasing on the receiving end are involved. In addition, it is a two-step stock transfer procedure. In a stock transfer without delivery, the following steps occur:

☐ The receiving plant enters an STO with the stock transport order type and U-item category.

☐ The STO is then used to plan the goods movement.

☐ The goods issue is posted to the STO in the issuing plant.

☐ The goods are posted as in-transit stock in the receiving plant with movement type 351.

☐ The stock is in the stock overview of the issuing plant with the *Release Stock Transport Order type*. Now select *Inventory Management > Goods Movement > Transfer Posting* from the menu.

☐ As soon as the stock is received at the receiving plant, the goods receipt is posted and the stock is changed from in-transit to unrestricted-use stock.

☐ The goods receipt is entered with reference to the PO by selecting *Inventory Management > Goods Movement > Goods Receipt > For Purchase Order* from the menu.

■ A stock transfer with delivery is done through shipping. Such a stock transfer can be achieved using a one-step or two-step transfer procedure. In this stock transfer, purchasing, shipping, and inventory management are involved. In a stock transfer with delivery through shipping, the following steps occur:

☐ The receiving plant enters an STO with the UB order type and the U-item category.

☐ Select *Purchasing > Purchase Order > Create > Stock Transfer* from the menu.

☐ The shipping point in the issuing plant enters a replenishment delivery in shipping.

☐ When the goods issue is posted, the material is assigned to the receiving plant for accounting purposes.

☐ A materials document and a financial accounting (FI) document are created.

☐ Select *Logistics > Sales and Distribution > Shipping and Transportation > Outbound Delivery > Create > Collective Processing of Documents Due for Delivery > Purchase Orders from the menu.*

☐ For a two-step procedure, select movement type 641.

☐ For a one-step procedure, select movement type 647. Note that in this case, the goods receipt does not need to be posted.

☐ As soon as the stock is received at the receiving plant, the goods receipt is posted and the stock is changed from in-transit to unrestricted-use stock.

☐ The goods receipt is entered with reference to the PO by selecting *Inventory Management > Goods Movement > Goods Receipt > For Purchase Order* from the menu.

41. How is stock transferred in a cross-company scenario?

■ Stocks can be transferred between plants that belong to different company codes. Such a stock transfer process can be done in any of the following ways:

☐ One-step plant-to-plant stock transfer

☐ Two-step plant-to-plant stock transfer

☐ STO without delivery through shipping

☐ STO with delivery through shipping

42. How can we post a goods issue in the case of an STO?

■ A goods issue indicates an outward movement of stocks from an issuing plant, that is, a decrease in stocks due to the removal of stocks from the issuing plant. The goods issue for an STO can be posted in Inventory Management or Shipping.

When the goods issue is posted in Inventory Management, the goods receipt can be posted with a reference to the STO. To post a goods issue in Inventory Management, perform the following steps:

- □ Select *Goods Movement > Transfer Posting in the Inventory Management* menu.
- □ Enter the issuing plant and the issuing storage location for the individual materials.
- □ Select movement type 351.

■ To post the goods issue in Shipping, perform the following steps:

- □ Select *Logistics > Logistics Execution > Outbound Process > Goods Issue for Outbound Delivery > Outbound Delivery > Create > Collective Processing of Documents Due for Delivery > Purchase Orders*. The PO tab now appears selected.
- □ Enter the necessary information on the Purchase Orders page.
- □ Select Execute. A list of deliveries is displayed.

■ The posting of the goods issue results in the following:

- □ During the creation of a material document for plants belonging to different company codes, an accounting document is also created.
- □ Creation of a goods issue slip.
- □ Decrease in the stocks in the issuing plant. The stocks are in transit to the receiving plant.
- □ Creation of posting lines on the accounts of the accounting system.
- □ An update of the consumption, reservation, and order.
- □ Creation of a transfer requirement when the Warehouse Management System manages the storage location.
- □ Creation of an inspection lot when inspection processing is connected.
- □ Creation of a PO history.

43.   How can we monitor stock in transit?

■ Stock in transit refers to the stock that is removed from the issuing plant but has not yet arrived at the receiving plant.

The stock in transit can be viewed and monitored by using the following approaches:

- □ *Stock overview*—To view the stock in transit by using stock overview, perform the following steps:
    - In the Inventory Management menu, select *Environment > Stock > Stock Overview*.
    - Select the material and the receiving plant.
    - Evaluate the stock overview of the selected plants.
    - Select a particular plant and detailed display. The stocks (including the stocks in transit) in the selected plant are displayed.

- □ *Plant stock availability list*—To view the stock in transit by using the plant stock availability list at the receiving plant, perform the following steps:
    - In the Inventory Management menu, select *Environment > Stock > Plant Stock* Availability.
    - Select the material and the receiving plant.
    - Enter the layout.
    - Evaluate the plant stock availability for the selected material. A list of the available stocks (including stocks in transit) is displayed.

44. How is a goods receipt entered in the receiving plant in the case of an STO?

- A goods receipt indicates the inward movement of goods at the receiving plant. When the goods issue is posted in Inventory Management and Shipping, the goods receipt can be posted in with reference to the STO. The goods receipt can be entered in the same way as the goods receipt is entered for a PO.

45. How can a stock transfer be monitored in Purchasing?

- A stock transfer can be monitored in Purchasing by using the following stock documents:
    - □ Purchase requisition
    - □ The STO
    - □ Stock transport scheduling agreement

46.   How is an STO created?

■ To create an STO, perform the following steps:

  ☐ Select *Purchase Order > Create > Vendor/Supplying Plant Known from the Purchasing menu.*

  ☐ Select order type UB for the STO and item category U for the stock transfer. Below Stock Transfer Using a Stock Transport Order, a table displaying the possible combinations of order type and item category appears.

  ☐ Enter the necessary data for all items.

  ☐ Save the STO.

47.   Define "source list."

■ The source list identifies the sources of a material that can and cannot be used for a certain plant within a predefined period. The sources in the source list are defined by means of a source list record.

48.   How do we generate a source list?

■ You can auto-generate a source list for an individual item or a group of items. Perform the following steps to generate a source list for a group of items:

  ☐ Select *Master Data > Source List > Follow-on Functions > Generate.*

  ☐ Enter the data.

  ☐ Select *Create the Source List.* A list of source records to be generated is displayed.

  ☐ Select the source list records you want to include in the source list.

  ☐ Select the Save icon (⊟) to save the selected source list records.

■ You can generate a source list for an individual item by performing the following steps:

  ☐ Select *Master Data > Source List > Maintain.*

  ☐ Enter the material number and plant number.

  ☐ Press Enter. The overview screen appears.

☐ Select *Edit > Generate Records.*

☐ Enter the validity period of the source list records that are to be created.

☐ Press Enter. The source list is created.

☐ Click the Save icon (⬛) to save the source list.

49. What are the different source determination procedures?

■ The different source determination procedures are as follows:

☐ *Quota arrangement*—In this procedure, if the system finds a quota arrangement for a material that is valid for a specified date, then the vendor who supplies this material is considered the source of supply.

☐ *Source list*—If the system does not find a quota arrangement for a material, then the system checks the entries in the source list. If there is a single preferred vendor for a source, then the system selects that vendor as the source. If there is more than one vendor on the source list, then the system lets the buyer select the preferred vendor.

☐ *Outline agreement and info records*—If there is no valid source list, then the system checks the contracts, agreements, and records for the materials. After the system checks, it provides a list, from which the buyer selects the vendor.

50. How does source determination work in the case of purchase requisitions?

■ The purchase requisitions are submitted to the normal MM source determination process to determine the source. If one of the sources is the default source, then automatic purchase requisition creation with source determination in SAP is possible. There is a list of vendors to select from and assign to the purchase requisition, depending on the customer location. If you have multiple vendors at the desired location, then you need to assign a source manually in the purchase requisition. If you have a fixed source, then check the indicator "fixed vendor" in the source list. The system will pick this source and assign it to purchase requisitions automatically.

51.   What are purchase requisitions as related to SAP?

■ Purchase requisitions in SAP describe a demand for both stock and non-stock items to the purchasing department. This can be done either automatically by the SAP system or manually. These purchase requisitions are converted to a PO by the procurement team or automatically by batch job and, finally, an order is sent to the vendor. You can see the purchase requisition process in Figure 4.1:

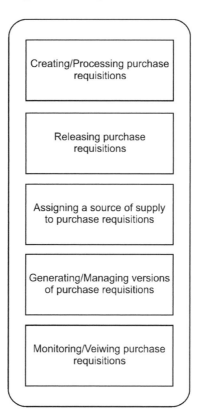

Figure 4.1: The Process of Purchase Requisition

52.   How can a purchase requisition be created?

■ Purchase requisitions can be created by using either of two approaches: direct or indirect. In the direct approach, employees of the requesting department enter a purchase requisition manually. The person creating the requisition finds out the details, such as what and how much to order and the delivery date. In the indirect approach, purchase requisition is initiated through another SAP component in various ways, such as materials planning and control, networks (from the SAP R/3 Project System (PS) component), maintenance orders (from the SAP R/3 Plant Maintenance (PM) and Service Management components), and production orders (from the Production Planning (PP) and Control components).

53. How can we create a purchase requisition with a material master record?

- You can create a purchase requisition with a material master record by using transaction code ME51N or performing the following steps:
  - □ Select *SAP Menu > Logistics > Materials Management > Purchasing > Purchase Requisition > Create*. The Create Purchase Requisition screen appears.
  - □ Enter the following details in the screen:
    - Material number of item or service
    - Quantity to be procured
    - Date of delivery for the material
    - Plant location of delivery
- The requisition process will copy the data into the purchase requisition screen.
- For a purchase requisition, the document type is important as it contains the internal and external number ranges used for requisitions. It also contains information about the valid item categories and the follow-on functions. SAP is delivered with two document types: NB for a standard purchase requisition and TB for a transport order.
  - □ You can configure a document type for the purchase requisition using the following navigation path: *IMG > Materials Management > Purchasing > Purchase Requisition > Define Document Types*.
  - □ Define a purchase requisition number, which is an attribute of the document type.
  - □ Select the source determination field in case the system needs to carry out an automatic source selection.

☐ Select an item category that allows the purchase requisition to follow the right path for the purchase requisition category.

☐ Configure the account assignment category, which determines the type of assignment data required for purchase requisition, by using the following navigation path: *IMG > Materials Management > Purchasing > Purchase Requisition > Account Assignment > Maintain Account Assignment Categories*.

☐ Enter the plant and storage location fields, if the location where the materials need to be shipped is known beforehand.

☐ Enter the purchasing group number, if it is not entered at the order level.

☐ Specify the requirement tracking number.

☐ Enter the requisitioner's name to search and order the purchase requisitions.

☐ Specify the plant that supplies the stock of materials in the case of a stock-transport order between plants.

54.   Can we generate a purchase requisition automatically?

■ You can generate a purchase requisition automatically only in a case where a material is sent out for external processing, for example subcontracting work. Another situation where you may need to generate a purchase requisition automatically is when the bill of materials is for a material other than a non-stock item.

55.   How can we create a purchase requisition without a material master record?

■ You can perform the following steps to create a purchase requisition without a material master record:

☐ Select *SAP Menu > Logistics > Materials Management > Purchasing > Purchase Requisition > ME51N–Create*. The *Create Purchase Requisition* screen appears.

☐ Enter the required data or change the existing data if needed.

☐ Press the Enter key. An overview of the item appears.

- Enter the following data in the respective fields:
  - Short text for the material, which is a short description of the material
  - Purchasing group key, which represents the purchasing group responsible for ordering the material (in the PGr column)
  - Account assignment category (in the A column)
  - Requested quantity (in the Quantity column)
  - Unit of measure (in the Unit column)
  - Delivery date (in the Deliv. Date column)
  - Material group (in the Matl. Group column)
  - Plant number (in the Plant column)
  - Storage location (in the Stor. Loc. column)
- Click the Item Details button. The Item Details screen appears.
- Select the Valuation tab in the Item Details screen.
- Now, specify price in the valuation price field for the material on the Item Details screen.
- Press the Enter key to enter additional account assignment information if the account assignment category selected is not U, which is unknown.
- Save the information entered for the purchase requisition.

56. How do we track a purchase requisition?

- You can track a purchase requisition using a tracking number entered by the requisitioner. You can use the transaction code MELB to select purchase requisitions by using the requisition tracking number. You can find this transaction using the following navigation path: *SAP Menu > Logistics > Materials Management > Purchasing > Purchase Requisition > List Displays > By Account Assignment > Transactions per Tracking Number.*

57. When can a purchase requisition be closed?

- A purchase requisition is closed when the requested amount of materials is equal to the amount purchased through a PO. A purchase requisition can be closed by setting the value of the indicator within the Item Details screen as closed.

- For closing a line item on a purchase requisition, the requisitioner must access the change-purchase-requisition transaction, ME52 or ME52N. The line item that must be flagged for deletion must be selected and the requisitioner must select *Edit > Delete*. After selecting this option, the delete indicator on the line item will be checked.

58.   State the configuration steps for a purchase requisition.

- The configuration steps for a purchase requisition are as follows:
  - □ Defining of document type
  - □ Processing time
  - □ Release procedure
  - □ Authorization check
  - □ Defining of the number ranges

59.   What are the important fields in a purchase requisition?

- The important fields in a purchase requisition are as follows:
  - □ Document type
  - □ Purchase requisition (number)
  - □ Source determination
  - □ Item category
  - □ Account assignment category
  - □ Delivery date
  - □ Plant
  - □ Storage location
  - □ Purchasing group
  - □ Material group
  - □ Requisition tracking number
  - □ Requisitioner
  - □ Supplying plant

60.   How do we change a purchase requisition once it is issued?

- To change a purchase requisition after it is issued, first check whether a PO was issued against it. If it was issued, then the purchase groups are informed. The next step is to check whether the purchase requisition is approved. If it is approved, then only limited changes are possible. Also, if the purchase requisition is created by the MRP, then much less interference in the process is possible. Keeping all these parameters regarding all the changes that are going to be brought into effect in mind, select the desired item and select *Go To > Statistics > Change Link*.

61. State the differences between the purchase requisition with a master record and without a master record.

■ In the case of a purchase requisition with a master record, the source list, information record, and vendor evaluation are present in the system. In this case, outline agreements are generated due to the change from a short-term purchasing to a long-term agreement. In the case of a purchase requisition with no material record, the material is ordered as a consumable item. The account assignment is done by specifying the consumption accounts against this acquisition. For example, the purchase information related to this requisition can be assigned to a specific cost center.

62. State the importance of the vendor evaluation in the purchase department.

■ The vendor evaluation is an important function of the purchase department as it helps optimize the procurement process by selecting vendors to supply materials or services.

63. What are the main criteria of the vendor evaluation?

■ The main criteria of the vendor evaluation are as follows:
  □ Price quality
  □ Delivery
  □ Service and support
  □ External service

64. How do we maintain the vendor evaluations in the MM module?

■ You can maintain the vendor evaluations in the MM module either by using the ME61 transaction code or by using the path: *SAP Menu > Logistics > Materials Management > Purchasing > Master Data > Vendor Evaluation > Maintain.*

65. What are the document types used in purchase requisitions?

■ Purchase requisitions are internal documents of an enterprise. These documents are used to request a particular material or service from the purchasing department of the enterpriser. The quantity of the requested material and the date of the procurement are also specified in the purchase requisitions. The document types used in purchase requisitions are as follows:
  □ Request for quotation (RFQ)
  □ Outline agreement
  □ PO

66. What is the difference between an indirectly created and directly created purchase requisition?

■ A purchase requisition is said to be created indirectly when it is initiated through another SAP component, such as consumption-based planning, the project system, plant maintenance, and production planning and control. On the other hand, a directly created purchase requisition is manually created through the requesting department. The creator has full control to decide the item, quantity to be ordered, and delivery date of the order.

67. Can a purchase requisition be manually generated through the reference of a PO or a scheduling agreement?

■ A purchase requisition cannot be generated by using the reference of a PO or by using a scheduling agreement.

68.   What is a PO? What does a PO contain?

- PO stands for Purchase Order and is a document that is issued by a buyer to a seller which consists of the type and quantity of the goods or services the seller will provide to the buyer at a specified date.
- A PO consists of:
  - □ *Document header*—Relates to the entire PO
  - □ *Number of items*—Relates to the number of items to be provided by the seller to the buyer.

69.   Where do we define payment terms in the PO?

- The payment terms in the PO represent the agreements of customers and vendors. You can define the payment terms in the PO in the master records of customers and vendors.

70.   What are the document types used in a PO?

- The document types used in a PO are:
  - □ Standard PO (NB)
  - □ STO (TB)
  - □ Framework order

71.   What is the difference between a blanket PO and a service order?

- A blanket PO is used for consumable materials, such as office paper. In the case of a blanket PO, no goods receipt is required. In a service order, the framework order document type is used for the PO and a goods receipt and service entry (SE) are required for the PO.

72.   What is price comparison?

- Price comparison is used to compare quotations from different vendors. You can use the transaction code ME49 to perform a price comparison between different vendors.

73. What are the document types used in scheduling agreements?

■ The document types used in scheduling agreements are:
  □ LP for standard scheduling agreements
  □ LT for stock transport scheduling agreements
  □ LPA for scheduling agreements with release documentation

74. What are the document types used in a contract?

■ The document types used in a contract are:
  □ Quantity contract—MK
  □ Value contract—WK

75. What is a contract?

■ A contract is an agreement between the customer and vendor that states that the vendor will supply material to the customer at an agreed price during a specified period of time. It can be based on either a total quantity or a total price. A contract avoids the need to create a new PO each time the material or service is required.

76. What are the different types of contracts?

■ A contract can be one of the following two types:
  □ *Quantity contract*—In this type of contract, the purchasing department has an agreement with the vendor for the supply of a specified quantity of materials or services.
  □ *Value contract*—In this type of contract, the purchasing department can limit with a vendor the total spending for a material. The release orders are valid only until the total spending for the value contract equals the total agreed-upon value.

77. What is the difference between a scheduling agreement and a contract?

■ A scheduling agreement contains the details of a delivery schedule, whereas a contract contains only quantity and price information and does not contain any details of specific delivery dates.

78. How can we create a contract?

■ You can create a contract using the transaction code ME31K or by performing the following steps:

  □ Select *SAP Menu > Logistics > Materials Management > Purchasing > Outline Agreement > Contract > Create*. The *Create Contract: Initial Screen* appears, which is quite similar to the initial screen for creating a scheduling agreement.

  □ Enter the agreement type field to ascertain the type of contract being created. The agreement types can be as follows:

    ▪ *WK*–Value contract

    ▪ *GCTR*–Value contract

    ▪ *MK*–Quantity contract

    ▪ *DC*–Distributed or centrally agreed contract

    ▪ *PCTR*–Value contract

  □ Enter the agreement date, name of the purchasing organization, and purchasing group information.

■ After entering these initial data, the transaction displays the header information that you are required to complete. When you submit these details, a contract is created.

79. Account assignment categories "U" and "X" can be used in purchase requisitions but not in POs. Why?

■ The account assignment categories "U" and "X" are used if you do not know the account assignment category for which a material is being procured. This type of account assignment category is allowed in a purchase requisition but not in a PO. This is because when the buyer creates a PO, the buyer has to select a valid account assignment category and maintain all valid account assignment details.

80. What is the difference in release procedure between internal documents and external documents?

■ The release procedure differs for internal and external documents. Internal documents and the purchase requisition can be released either at the item level or at the header level. Additionally, internal documents can be released either with classification or without classification. External documents, such as the PO or a request for a quotation, can only be released at the header level by the classification method.

81. Define "procurement cycle."

■ The procurement cycle for materials in SAP MM consists of the following segments:
  □ Determination of requirements
  □ Source determination
  □ Vendor selection and comparison of quotations
  □ PO processing
  □ PO follow-up
  □ Goods receiving and inventory management
  □ Invoice verification
  □ Payment processing
■ Figure 4.2 displays each of these segments:

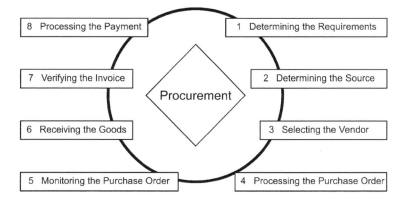

Figure 4.2: Procurement Cycle

Now we'll discuss the individual segments of the procurement cycle.

Determination of Requirements

■ The requirements for a material in a company or organization is identified either in the user departments or materials planning and control department. The materials planning and control department deals with both proper MRP and the demand-based approach to inventory control. The day-to-day checking of the stock levels of materials is maintained by the master records by using the order-point method. The purchase requisitions can be created manually or they can be generated in an automated order by the materials planning and control system.

Source Determination

■ The source is determined on the basis of past orders and existing longer-term purchase agreements. This helps in creating RFQs electronically, with the help of SAP electronic data interchange (EDI) if required.

Vendor Selection and Comparison of Quotations

■ The SAP system can simulate pricing scenarios for different vendors. It also allows you to compare quotations given by different vendors. The best quotation is selected and rejection letters can be sent automatically to the vendors whose quotations are rejected.

Purchase Order Processing

■ The purchasing system collects information from the purchase requisition and the quotations and helps create a PO. With the help of the purchase requisitions, you can generate POs by yourself; otherwise, the system generates them automatically. Vendor scheduling agreements and contracts (contracts are a type of longer-term purchase agreement in the SAP system) are also supported in PO processing.

Purchase Order Follow-Up

■ After PO processing, follow-up is required to keep track of the POs. The system checks the reminder periods that have been specified and automatically prints reminders at predefined time intervals. In addition, it provides an updated status of all purchase requisitions, quotations, and POs.

Goods Receipt and Inventory Management

■ A goods receipt is confirmed by the employees of the goods department by simply entering the PO number.

Invoice Verification

- The SAP system supports the checking and verification of invoices. An employee of the invoice verification department is notified of quantity and price discrepancies, because the system has access to PO and goods receipt data. This, in turn, speeds up the process of auditing and clearing invoices for payment.

Payment Processing

- Once an invoice is verified, the payment is processed for the respective vendor by the SAP system.

82. What are the main documents used in MM?

- The following are the main documents used in MM:
  - ☐ Purchase requisitions
  - ☐ POs
  - ☐ Goods transfers
  - ☐ Goods receipts
  - ☐ Goods issues

83. What are the various steps of the MM cycle?

- The following are the different steps of the MM cycle:
  - ☐ Create material
  - ☐ Create vendor
  - ☐ Assign material to vendor
  - ☐ Procure raw material by using purchase requisition
  - ☐ Locate a vendor for a certain material
  - ☐ Process goods receipts
  - ☐ Goods issue
  - ☐ Invoice verification

84. What is the definition of procurement?

- Procurement can be defined as the purchase of goods or services at the best possible total cost in the correct amount and quality. It is the process of acquiring goods and services and covers acquisitions from both third parties and from in-house providers.

85. What is the account assignment category in a PO document?

■ The account assignment category plays an important role in purchasing documents. It contains many control functions that help to determine the objects that are charged in the case of an ordered material. The ordered material must be procured for direct usage or consumption. With the help of the account assignment category in the purchasing documents, the cost of the material can be allocated to a single controlling object or it can be allocated among various controlling objects.

86. What is the difference between a PO and a purchase requisition?

■ A PO is a document type that notifies you about formal requests for materials or services from an outside vendor or plant. A purchase requisition is a document type that notifies you about a need for materials or services.

87. What is the creation indicator?

■ The creation indicator defines whether the planned orders, purchase requisitions, or schedule lines must be created for materials that are procured externally. It also defines whether or not MRP lists need to be created.

88. What is the automatic generation of POs from purchase requisitions?

■ The SAP system can automatically convert purchase requisitions into POs. This task can be performed either online or in the background. In the process of conversion, the SAP system attempts to merge as many purchase requisition items as possible to form one PO. Automatic generation of POs from purchase requisitions is recommended only in cases when you have a well-maintained SAP system, otherwise manual processing is advised.

89.   What is a quotation?

■ A quotation is offered by a vendor to a purchasing organization and contains details regarding the supply of materials or performance of services subject to specified conditions. A quotation is a legal document that binds the vendor for a certain period. It is created by the vendor in response to a request for a quotation issued by the purchasing organization. A quotation contains all of the details about an order, such as the total quantity and delivery date of a material or service offered.

90.   How do we enter a quotation from a vendor in the SAP system?

■ Quotations should be entered into the SAP system at the proper time because of deadlines attached with each RFQ. You can enter a quotation from a vendor into the SAP system either by using the transaction code ME47 or by following the path: *SAP Menu > Logistics > Materials Management > Purchasing > RFQ/Quotation > Quotation > ME47-Maintain.*

91.   How can we compare price factors in quotations?

■ You can compare price factors either by using the ME49 transaction code or by following the path: *SAP Menu > Logistics > Materials Management > Purchasing > RFQ/Quotation > Price Comparison.* A screen appears where you can make a comparison among different quotations. Quotation selection is made on the basis of certain factors, such as purchasing organization, vendor, material, or collective RFQ number.

■ Other criteria for comparing price factors in quotations are as follows:

  □ *Reference quotation*—All other quotations are compared with this quotation. If the reference quotation is missing then the quotations are compared to each other.

☐ *Mean value quotation*—The mean value quotation is the average of all the individual quotations. If this value is set, then all the comparisons are made with respect to the average price of the quotations.

☐ *Minimum value quotation*—If this value is set, all the comparisons are made with respect to the lowest price of the quotation.

☐ *Percentage basis*—This allows the user to specify which value is used as the 100% basis. Value can be the mean price, maximum price, or the minimum price.

■ In addition to the preceding criteria, the following price comparison criteria indicators can also be set:

☐ *Include discounts*—If this indicator is set, then at the time of quotation the comparison includes price discounts offered by the vendor. If this indicator is not set, then no discounts are included in the comparison process.

☐ *Include delivery costs*—If this indicator is set, then for any price comparisons at the time of the quotation, the delivery costs are included in the price. The delivery cost includes freight costs, duty levied, or some procurement costs, such as packing, insurance, and handling.

☐ *Determine effective price*—This is set if cash discounts and delivery costs are implied in the price comparison.

92. What are the qualitative factors that can prove advantageous to the client while bidding?

■ The following are the qualitative factors that can prove advantageous to the client while bidding:

☐ *Previous relationship with client*—If the bidder and the client have a good relationship with each other, this will be taken into account while making the final decision on the bid winner.

☐ *Compliance with the Equal Opportunity Act*—Many clients insist that equal employment opportunity laws be followed while comparing quotations.

☐ *Strategic alliances*—Strategic alliances among trading partners also play a major role in deciding the bid winner. For instance, consider that bidding is going on for the Linux Server and company A comes out with the lowest bid among its competitors, companies B and C. However, if the client is entertaining a sound strategic alliance with company B, it will place the bid with B, in spite of the fact that company A's bid value is the lowest one.

☐ *Minority-owned and female-owned businesses*—Some clients also give preference to businesses that are minority-owned or female-owned and assign them contracts and POs accordingly. If the client has indicated any such preference in the RFQ, this can play a key role in choosing the bid winner.

☐ *Warranty and return process*—The warranty period for an item and the return policy of a bidder are very important parameters for the purchaser. Usually, in the case of Request for Quote (RFQ) of products, the purchaser opts for a bidder who offers a lesser price per unit. However, in the case of personal computers, the warranty period offered, rather than price, is considered a deciding factor. The case is the same with the return policy.

☐ *Creative pricing*—In some situations, it is not possible to assign the best price with respect to the RFQ. The purchasing department is responsible for looking for ways to reduce the cost.

93.   How can we reject a quotation?

■ You can reject a quotation in the system by simply typing the command ME47 or following the path: *SAP Menu > Logistics > Materials Management > Purchasing > RFQ/Quotation > Quotation > Maintain*. As a result, a screen appears. Here, you can enter the RFQ number of the quotation that is to be rejected. Then the line is selected and is flagged in the Rejected column (with the letter R) to signify that the quotation is rejected.

94.   What is an RFQ?

■ RFQ stands for Request for Quotation or Request for Quote. An RFQ is a document sent to a vendor by a purchasing organization. The vendor sends quotations with prices in response. An RFQ consists of two parts:

☐ *RFQ header*—Contains general information, for example, the name and address of the vendor.

□ *Items*—Contains information about the total quantities and delivery dates for the materials or services specified in the RFQ.

95. How are RFQs and quotations processed in SAP?

■ RFQs and quotations are processed in the following manner in SAP:

□ RFQs are created either manually or by using an already existing RFQ, requisition, or outline purchase agreement by the company.

□ The company creates a list of vendors who are to receive the RFQ. For this purpose, a separate document is created for each vendor.

□ The company enters the prices and conditions set out in the quotation submitted by the vendor into the RFQ document.

□ The company carries out a comparative appraisal of all of the vendor quotations by means of the price comparison list. The quotations given by each vendor are compared item by item. The mean value quotation represents the average value of the individual quotes.

□ The company enters the most favorable quotation in an info record and sends rejection letters to the other, unsuccessful bidders.

□ Finally, the company monitors the status of follow-on activities related to the RFQ and quotation (e.g., a contract is set up or a PO is issued).

96. How can an RFQ be created?

■ RFQs can be created in any of the following ways:

□ *Manual approach*—Data for an RFQ is entered manually for the materials for which you wish prices to be quoted.

□ *Copying approach*—An RFQ is copied from an existing RFQ.

□ *Referencing approach*—An RFQ is created by using reference requisitions or an outline purchase agreement.

□ *Automatic approach*—An RFQ is created automatically by using a requisition.

97. What transaction codes are used in RFQs?

■ The following transaction codes are used in RFQs:
  - □ ME41—Creates an RFQ
  - □ ME42—Changes an RFQ
  - □ ME43—Displays an RFQ
  - □ ME44—Maintains an RFQ supplement
  - □ ME45—Releases an RFQ

98. How can we create an RFQ in the SAP system?

■ An RFQ can be created either by typing the transaction code ME41 or by following the navigation path: *SAP Menu > Logistics > Materials Management > Purchasing > RFQ/Quotation > ME41-Create.*

99. What is the RFQ type?

■ The RFQ type is a two-character field used in the configuration of RFQ document types. It helps the company to differentiate between the different types of RFQs that they can send out.

100. List the important key fields for RFQs.

■ Important key fields for RFQs are as follows:
  - □ RFQ date
  - □ Quotation deadline
  - □ RFQ document number
  - □ Organizational data
  - □ Default data for items
  - □ Collective number
  - □ Validity start/validity end
  - □ Application by
  - □ Binding period
  - □ Reference data
  - □ RFQ item detail
  - □ RFQ delivery schedule

□ Additional data

□ Vendor selection

101. What is the RFQ delivery schedule?

■ The RFQ delivery schedule refers to the information entered by the purchaser that is comprised of the date, time, and amount required. You can access the delivery scheduling screen by pressing the SHIFT+F5 key combination from the keyboard in the SAP interface.

102. How can we release an RFQ?

■ You can follow this navigation path to release an *RFQ: SAP Menu > Logistics > Materials Management > Purchasing > RFQ/ Quotation > ME45-Release.* A screen appears; enter all the information on the screen and the RFQ is released based on the information entered.

103. What is the purchasing document category for an RFQ?

■ The purchasing document category for an RFQ is the single character A. For other documents, such as POs, the category is F, for contracts it is K, and for scheduling agreements it is L.

104. How can we find the list of vendors to send an RFQ?

■ You can use the information record to find the list of the materials; from there, you can find out the vendors from whom the goods have been purchased in the past. Thereafter, the request for purchase requisition is issued. Alternatively, you can go for a source list.

105. What is the role of the confirmation control key?

■ The confirmation control key is used to specify whether a notification for shipping is expected for a PO item.

106. What is a purchasing document?

■ A purchasing document is a document type used by the purchasing department to procure materials or services.

107. What are the various transaction codes used in Materials Management Purchasing (MM-PUR)?

■ The following transaction codes are used in MM-PUR:

Transaction	Purpose
ME53N	Displays the purchase requisition
MN06	Displays a PO message
ME03	Displays the source list
ME23N	Displays the PO
ME13	Displays the info record
ME43	Displays an RFQ
ME62	Displays the vendor evaluation
ME48	Displays quotations
ME33K	Displays contracts
ME33L	Displays scheduling agreements
MEQ3	Displays quota arrangements
MN03	Displays an RFQ message
MN26	Displays an inbound delivery message

108. Name some of the data points provided by purchasing for the materials.

■ Some of the data points provided by purchasing for the materials are the base unit of measure, purchasing group, remainder days, shipping instructions, tolerance levels, goods receipt processing time, critical parts, and just-in-time (JIT) schedule indications.

109. What are the external purchasing documents available in the standard SAP system?

■ The external purchasing documents available in the standard SAP system are as follows:

□ *RFQ*—Transmitted to a vendor by a purchasing organization. The vendor sends quotations with prices in response.

□ *Quotation*—Offered by a vendor to a purchasing organization. It contains the details regarding the supply of materials or performance of services subject to specified conditions.

□ *PO*—Order given by purchasing organization to a vendor to request supply of materials or services.

□ *Contract*—A type of outline agreement or longer-term buying arrangement in terms of SAP MM. The contract is a necessary assurance given by a vendor to ensure they will procure a material or service over a certain period of time.

□ *Scheduling agreement*—Similar to a contract, a scheduling agreement is also a type of outline agreement or longer-term buying arrangement. It facilitates creation of delivery schedules by specifying purchase quantities, delivery dates, and precise time of delivery over a predefined period.

110. How does the SAP system differentiate between purchasing documents?

■ Document type is the unit used to differentiate between different kinds of purchasing documents in the SAP system. Each document has a unique number that determines the significant number range and the fields that are offered to you for data maintenance purposes.

111. How are purchasing documents numbered?

■ In the SAP system, each document is assigned a unique number. These numbers can also be alphanumeric. You can assign these numbers in two ways, either internally or externally, depending on the policy of your company or enterprise. An internal number is one that the SAP system assigns automatically, whereas an external number is one that the person creating the document must supply manually. Alphanumeric assignment of numbers is only possible in the latter case.

112. What is meant by PO, as related to SAP? What are the different ways a PO can be created in SAP?

- ■ A PO is a request made by a purchaser to a vendor (or supplier) to deliver a specified quantity of goods or services. In addition to the quantity of goods and services, a PO includes the following information:
  - □ Type of goods and services
  - □ Price of goods and services
  - □ Time specified by the purchaser to deliver the goods and services.
  - □ Terms and conditions of payment for the goods and services
- ■ The PO can be created by the following ways:
  - □ *Vendor known*—This procedure is used when you know the vendor from whom you receive the order.
  - □ *Vendor unknown*—This procedure is used when you want the system to select and suggest possible vendors. These suggestions are made on the basis of sources of supply (purchase agreement, info records, and source lists) already stored in the system.
  - □ *Creation of POs from the assigned requisitions*—This procedure is used when requisitions that have already been assigned to a vendor need to be listed for a purchasing group.
  - □ *Stock transfer*—This procedure is used when you order the material from one of your plants and not from a vendor.
  - □ *Vendor managed inventory (VMI)*—This procedure is used when you want to create the PO from the acknowledgement received from the vendor through EDI.

113. How can we create a PO automatically?

■ A PO can be created automatically in Purchasing and in Inventory Management:

  ☐ *Creating a PO automatically in Purchasing*—To create a PO automatically from a purchase requisition, you need to activate the auto-PO indicator for the material master and also for the vendor master. You can create the purchase requisition by using the transaction code ME51 or ME51N.

  ☐ *Creating a PO automatically in Inventory Management*—For creating the PO automatically in Inventory Management, you must define one of the purchase organizations as the standard purchase organization. In addition, assign your plant to the standard purchase organization, maintain the purchasing information record along with the price, maintain the indicator for movement types 101 & 161, and define the default values (MB01) for the document type.

■ After entering and posting the goods receipt without entering the PO number, a PO is created automatically.

114. How can we create POs with known and unknown vendors?

■ You can create a PO with a known or unknown vendor by using the ME21N or ME25 transaction codes, respectively. You can also create a PO with a known or unknown vendor by performing the following steps:

  ☐ Select *SAP Menu > Logistics > Materials Management > Purchasing > Purchase Order > Create*.

  ☐ Double-click *ME21N–Vendor/Supplying Plant Known* to create a PO with a known vendor. The *Create Purchase Order* screen appears where you can create a PO.

  ☐ Double-click *ME25–Vendor Unknown* to create a PO with an unknown vendor. The *Create Purchase Order: Initial Screen* appears where a PO can be created.

115. Can a line item in a PO be blocked after it has been created?

■ Yes, a line item in a PO can be blocked after it has been created. Blocking a line item stops acceptance of any goods receipts related to that line item.

116. How can we cancel a PO line item?

■ You can cancel a PO line item by using the ME22N transaction code. You can also cancel a PO item by performing the following steps:

☐ Select *SAP Menu > Logistics > Materials Management > Purchasing > Purchase Order*.

☐ Double-click *ME22N–Change*. The *Display Purchase Order* screen appears, where you can cancel the PO line item.

117. What are the account assignment categories in a PO?

■ SAP provides you with a number of account assignment categories that you can use for a PO. An account assignment category indicates the account assignment details that are required for an item.

118. Can multiple accounts be assigned to a PO line?

■ Yes, you are allowed to assign multiple accounts to one PO line. Multiple account assignments may be required in a situation where the cost of the item to be purchased is divided among multiple people.

119. What is an outline purchase agreement? What are the types of outline purchase agreements?

■ An outline purchase agreement is a long-term agreement between the purchasing department and a vendor for supply of materials and services for a given period of time. The purchase department negotiates a set of terms and conditions with the vendor, and these terms and conditions remain fixed for the period of agreement. The agreement does not contain any information on specific delivery dates. An outline purchase agreement can be one of the following two types:

- □ *Contract*—In this type of agreement, release orders can be issued for materials or services when the customer requires them.

- □ *Scheduling agreement*—In this type of agreement, the purchasing department makes arrangements to procure materials according to a schedule agreed upon between the purchasing department and the vendor.

120. What is an item category? What will happen if we use the consignment item category in SAP? What will happen if we use the subcontracting item category in a PO?

- ■ An item category is an important field in the purchasing document. The item category determines whether or not an ordered item requires a material number or an account assignment or requires a goods receipt and/or an invoice receipt, or if it is to be placed in stock.

- ■ Item categories are also used in categorizing the different types of stocks (including the special stocks available in the standard SAP solution) and the types of procurement processes.

- ■ If we use the consignment item category in SAP, the items are procured on a consignment basis and the account assignments cannot be made for those materials that are ordered on the consignment. The consignment stocks are not valuated and are managed separately.

121. What are the different types of item category?

- ■ An item category is a field in purchase requisition that specifies the category of purchase requisition. The following are the different types of item categories:
  - □ Blank—Standard
  - □ K—Consignment
  - □ L—Subcontracting
  - □ S—Third party

☐ D—Service

☐ U—Stock transfer

122. What is an account assignment category? How is it configured?

■ An account assignment category ascertains the type of accounting assignment information that is required for purchase requisition. Examples of account assignments include cost centers, general ledger accounts, cost objects, and assets. You can configure account assignment categories by using the following navigation path: *IMG > Materials Management > Purchasing > Purchase Requisition > Account Assignment > Maintain Account Assignment Categories.*

123. What is a scheduling agreement? How can it be created?

■ A scheduling agreement is an outline purchase agreement between the purchasing department and a vendor where the vendor supplies materials to the customer at a specified time and date. This type of outline purchase agreement is useful for customers who supply materials on a regular basis. A scheduling agreement can be created either manually or with reference to purchase requisitions, quotations, or contracts. You can create a scheduling agreement either by using the transaction code ME31L or by performing the following steps:

☐ Select *SAP Menu > Logistics > Materials Management > Purchasing > Outline Agreement > Scheduling Agreement > Create.*

☐ Double-click *ME31L–Vendor Known.* The *Create Scheduling Agreement: Initial Screen* appears where you can create a scheduling agreement.

124. How can we create a scheduling agreement with a reference?

■ You can create a scheduling agreement with reference to a purchase requisition, quotation, or contract either by using the transaction code ME31L or by performing the following steps:

◻ Select *SAP Menu > Logistics > Materials Management > Purchasing > Outline Agreement > Scheduling Agreement > Create.*

◻ Double-click *ME31L–Vendor Known.* The *Create Scheduling Agreement: Initial Screen* appears. On this screen, you are provided with options to reference a purchase requisition, quotation, or contract while creating your scheduling agreement.

125. What are the allowed account assignment categories in a PO?

■ The possible categories of account assignment in a PO are:

◻ *Account assignment A (assets)*—This account assignment is used to order fixed asset items.

◻ *Account assignment K (cost center)*—This account assignment is used to order an expense item (goods or services).

◻ *Account assignment ' ' (for inventory)*—This account assignment is used to order inventory.

126. What is service procurement?

■ Service procurement consists of activities such as bidding, contract management, and operational procurement processes, from requisition to payment.

127. What is the mandatory data that we must enter while creating a PO?

■ You need the following data before creating a new PO:

◻ *Delivery date*—A desired delivery date is required when creating a PO. If the delivery date field is empty, the system automatically determines the delivery date as the current date plus the planned delivery time for the material.

□ *Account assignment*—The account assignment category and the account assignment data, such as the number of the cost center to be charged, are required.

□ *Material number*—The number is required for the material that is to be ordered, if a material master record is defined for the material. When no material master record is defined for the material, you need a short description of the material, the account assignment, and the material group.

□ *MPN material number*—The manufacturer part number (MPN) material number is required when you want to order the material with an MPN.

□ *Plant*—You need the plant code for which the material or service is to be ordered.

□ *Number assignment*—You must have a PO number if your company uses external number assignment. The PO number must fall within the permitted number range.

□ *Price*—The net price of the material is required.

□ *Vendor*—A vendor master record number is required.

128. Where can we maintain the conditions in the PO?

■ We can maintain the conditions in the PO at the following levels:

□ The conditions can be maintained on the entire PO.

□ The conditions can be maintained in a particular item of the material to be supplied and, in the case of services, conditions can be maintained in the set of service specifications.

□ The conditions can be maintained at the service line level for individual services (tasks or activities).

129. What is the difference between procurement for stock and procurement for consumption?

■ In procurement for stock, when you order a material, the system does not require an account assignment because the posting to the appropriate stock and consumption occurs automatically every time transactions related to goods take place.

■ In procurement for consumption, you need to enter the account assignment (such as cost center) that specifies the purpose of consumption. Upon receipt of goods, the material or service is shown as having been consumed.

130. What is the difference between external procurement and internal procurement?

■ In external procurement, the procurement of raw material, trading goods, and services is made from an external supplier for the organizational units of an enterprise that need the items or services.

■ In internal procurement, the procurement of raw material, trading goods, and services is made from an organizational unit of an enterprise for other organizational units of the same enterprise that need the items or services.

131. What is a document type?

■ A document type is used to differentiate between different kinds of purchasing documents. In other words, different purchasing documents are distinguished on the basis of their document types. Document types are defined for RFQs, POs, and contracts.

132. What are the ways of converting planned orders into purchase requisitions?

■ You can convert the planned orders into purchase requisitions either by converting them individually or by collectively converting all the planned orders.

133. What transaction code is used to convert planned orders into requisitions in MRP?

■ The OPPR transaction code is used to convert planned orders into requisitions in MRP.

134. Can we add custom fields to POs and RFQs?

■ Yes, you can add custom fields to POs and RFQs.

135. What are the external purchasing documents and internal purchasing documents used in MM?

■ A purchasing document is like an instrument used to procure materials or services. The following are the external purchasing documents:

  □ *RFQ*—Contains the requirements defined in a requisition for a material or service and is sent to the vendor.

  □ *Quotation*—Contains a vendor's prices and conditions and is the basis for vendor selection.

  □ *PO*—A request made by a purchaser to a vendor (or supplier) to deliver a specified quantity of goods or services.

  □ *Contract*—Helps release orders for agreed materials or services depending on the requirement of the purchasing organization.

  □ *Scheduling agreement*—Contains a list of items in which the type of procurement of each item is defined.

■ The purchase requisition is an internal purchasing document use to note the requirements of material or services and also to track such requirements. A purchase requisition is an internal document; it cannot be used outside the enterprise.

136. How is a framework order (FO) different from a standard PO?

■ An FO is a purchasing document used for procuring materials or services. This type of PO has an extended validity period instead of a stipulated delivery date as in the case of the standard PO.

137. What document types can be used in cases of service procurement?

■ Service procurement is used by organizations to procure services or parts of services. It consists of activities such as bidding, contract management, and all the activities from requisition to payment.

138. What is the procurement type? What are the procurement types used in SAP?

- With the help of the procurement type indicator, the system can easily define whether the material is to be procured through internal production or external procurement, or through both.
- The following are the procurement types used for internal production:
  - □ Phantom assemblies
  - □ Production in an alternative plant
  - □ Withdrawal from an alternative plant
  - □ Direct production
- The following are the methods available for external procurement:
  - □ Consignment
  - □ Subcontracting
  - □ Stock transfer

139. Why should we use multiple account assignment in a PO?

- Using multiple account assignment in a PO allows you to apportion the cost associated with a PO item. When you use multiple account assignment, the account assignment data takes the form of individual account assignment items.

140. How is the Stock Transport Order (STO) different from the standard PO?

- In the STO, the UB document type is used; STO also requires a supplying plant for the movement of materials. In the standard PO, the NB document type is used and requires a vendor for the procurement of material.

141. How can we return a material that we have received with reference to a PO?

■ In the case of an external vendor, when your company returns a good received with reference to a PO, the reference of the PO is not mandatory in order to post the return in the system. The system will post a goods receipt correction and issue a credit memo against the vendor. However, if the vendor is internal, you may need the PO reference. In this case, the system automatically updates the stock, without any internal billing.

142. How are free items managed in a PO?

■ Mark the item as "free" in the PO. The price for such PO items will be zero.

143. Which documents are used as references when we create a PO?

■ At the time of creating a PO, we take the reference of the purchase requisition, RFQ, and any other POs. However, it is not necessary to take the reference of these documents as most of the values are automatically taken by the SAP R/3 software.

144. Suppose we want to procure a material using a PO and intend to accept delivery of the material at different times. In addition, if such material has a graduated discount scale, how would we proceed to take advantage of the discount arrangement?

■ Perform the following steps to do this:
  □ First, you must enter the required order items that have the same material code but different delivery dates.
  □ Enter each order item with its unique material number and also enter the materials information into its related accounts.
  □ Create a schedule line by entering an order item with its respective material number.

☐ Now, create POs with different delivery dates and enter them in the SAP system.

☐ You will then be able to create PO units different from each other and take advantage of the discount arrangement on each of the POs.

145. Explain the significance of the PO price unit. In addition, what should we note in case of a goods receipt?

■ The PO price unit describes the measurement unit (such as liter, day, or degree) of the material in which it is ordered. It is stored either in the purchasing info record or material master record. This measurement unit in the PO helps the SAP system to create a relationship between the PO price unit and the PO unit conversion that, in turn, helps the SAP system to calculate the PO unit price automatically.

■ At the time of receiving goods, you must enter both the quantity in the PO unit and the quantity in the PO price unit. The system will automatically calculate the quantity in the PO price unit, and then you will have to check the calculated quantity against the actual quantity. If there is any difference, you need to change it manually. This procedure for evaluating material is followed at the time of invoice verification also.

146. What is the transaction code to set price control for receipts (goods/invoice)?

■ The transaction code OMW1 is used to set price control for receipts (goods/invoice).

147. What is the outline agreement? What is the difference between a contract and a scheduling agreement?

■ The outline agreement refers to a deal between the purchasing organization and the vendor to deliver materials or services. The outline agreement also contains all the terms and conditions to be followed at the time of the transaction between the purchasing organization and the vendor. This outline agreement is a long-term agreement between the purchasing organization and the vendor. A contract is a part of the outline agreement, which helps release orders for agreed-upon materials or services depending on the requirements of the purchasing organization.

■ The scheduling agreement is procurement of materials at a defined time interval or date. The scheduling agreement contains a list of items where the type of procurement of each item is defined. The type of procurement can be standard, subcontracting, consignment, and stock transfer.

148. What is the difference between quantity and value contracts?

■ *Quantity contracts*—The quality contract is used when the total quantity to be ordered is known in advance during the validity period. This contract is considered fulfilled when release orders of the given total quantity have been issued.

■ *Value contracts*—The value contract is used when the total value of the release orders does not exceed a definite and predefined value. The contract is considered fulfilled when release orders of the given total the value have been issued.

149. What is a centrally agreed contract?

■ A centrally agreed contract type is created without specifying the name of the plant. The plant specification is provided at the time of creating the contract release order. In a centrally agreed contract, different conditions for individual plants can be easily maintained. Moreover, different ordering addresses or goods suppliers in the vendor master record can also be specified in this type of contract. The centrally agreed contract is useful in enterprises that have a central purchasing department and in which materials need to be bought for different plants. In this case, they create a high-level contract used by the other department-specific purchase organizations within the enterprise. The use of such centrally agreed contracts usually results in more favorable conditions of purchase and helps maintain consistency in process of purchasing throughout the enterprise.

150. What is a service master record?

■ A service master record is a document that contains information about the service. You can access the service master record by using the AC03 transaction code. The menu path for accessing the service master record is: *SAP Menu > Logistics > Materials Management > Service Master > Service > Service Master.*

151. List the important fields of a service master record.

■ The important fields of a service master record are as follows:
   □ *Service number*—Defined for external or internal numbering of the service
   □ *Service category*—Distinguishes between the types of services
   □ *Descriptive text*—Contains a short or long description of the service
   □ *Base unit of measurement*—Contains the unit in which you can measure the service
   □ *Material/service group*—Allows the service to be selected for grouping purposes
   □ *Valuation class*—Finds the general ledger accounts that are related to the services

152. What is a standard service catalog (SSC)?

■ An SSC is a general standardized catalog that contains detailed explanations of services. The descriptions of these services are stored as master records and help to remove data duplication.

153. How can the services be purchased?

■ The services can be purchased by first creating a document in the system that forms the base of the purchasing process. This document can be a purchase requisition, an RFQ, or a PO. Next, determine the possible sources that can provide the service. For this, you can either select a new service or a service that has been previously used. If the service is requested for the first time, a bid invitation process is started. In the bid invitation process, you first need to create an RFQ and then record the incoming quotations in it. The best quotation is determined based upon certain factors, such as price and warranty period. The order is then sent to the successful bidder, who receives either a standard PO or a release order issued against an existing contract.

154. What is a service entry sheet?

- A service entry sheet is a transaction in which the data related to the service that has been ordered is recorded using a PO. You can use the ML81N transaction code to locate the service entry sheet. You can also locate the service entry sheet by using the following path: *SAP Menu > Logistics > Materials Management > Service Entry Sheet > Maintain.*

155. What is a blanket PO? How can it be created?

- A PO that has a validity period and contains a simple process of procuring materials or services is referred to as a blanket PO. To create a blanket PO, use the ME21 or ME21N transaction code.

156. What is a distributed contract?

- A distributed contract is issued after creating the centrally agreed contract. It is issued by a central purchasing organization to their local purchasing organizations. The local purchasing organizations use the conditions specified in the distributed contract for the procurement of materials or external services. Using the distributed contract, the local purchasing organization creates release orders and sends copies of the release orders back to the central processing organization.

- The distributed contract enables the local purchasing department to benefit from the terms created and agreed upon centrally, which in turn helps them to order services or materials on better terms. The release orders created on the basis of a centrally agreed contract (distributed locally) can be sent directly to the vendors or agencies. The central purchasing organization stores all central and local release orders.

157. What are the allowed item categories used with contracts?

- The item categories used with contracts are based on the materials issued and are as follows:
  - □ *Item category M*—Use this category when an unknown material is issued
  - □ *Item category W*—Use this category when the value and quantity of materials are unknown
  - □ *Item category D*—Use this category when you procure an external service
  - □ *Item category K*—Use this category when a consignment material is involved
  - □ *Item category L*—Use this category when a subcontracting material is involved

158. How can we create a scheduling agreement in SAP?

- You can create a scheduling agreement in SAP either manually or by using the referencing techniques. To create a scheduling agreement manually, you must enter all the information on the scheduling agreement manually. You can use reference documents from where you will copy the information related to the scheduling agreement. These reference documents can be purchase requisitions, RFQs, and centrally agreed contracts.

159. What are schedule lines?

- Schedule lines are generally created adjacent to the schedule agreements. For example, suppose you have a material that is procured through a subcontract and you are required to ensure the delivery of this material on specific days. For this, you can create a schedule line for the scheduling agreement of that material. In the source list of the schedule line, you must provide information regarding the vendor and sheduling agreement along with the validity dates of delivery and also specify the agreement.

160. How can we create a schedule line for a scheduling agreement?

- *Creating schedule lines*—To create delivery schedule lines for a scheduling agreement item, you are required to have the following information:
  - □ The number of scheduling agreements
  - □ The number of all the items that need to be scheduled
  - □ A list of the delivery dates, times, and quantities you have negotiated with the vendor
- After gathering the above information, you must perform the following steps to create a delivery schedule line for a scheduling agreement:
  - □ Select *Outline Agreement > Scheduling Agreement > Delivery Schedule > Maintain*.
- The initial screen for the creation of delivery schedules under scheduling agreements appears.
  - □ Provide the document number of the scheduling agreement.
  - □ Press the Enter key.
- The screen displaying an item overview for which the scheduling agreement is created appears.
  - □ Select the item you are required to schedule.
  - □ Select *Item > Delivery Schedule*.
  - □ Enter the following information for each schedule line:
    - Date category (month, week, or day) and the corresponding date
    - Delivery time spot (if applicable)

- Quantity to be delivered (the unit of measure is the same as in the scheduling agreement)
- Now, you must add a purchase requisition reference. Perform the following steps to do this:
  - □ Select *Schedule > Agreement > Schedule > Create New*.
  - □ Add a reference to the purchase requisition to get the delivery data from an existing requisition.
  - □ Save the delivery schedule.
  - □ The scheduling agreement delivery schedule is now created in the SAP system. In order for the information in the delivery schedule to be transmitted to the vendor, the system generates a message for the schedule.

161. How is a scheduling agreement release sent to a vendor?

- You send a scheduling agreement release to the vendor as a forecast delivery schedule. By doing this, you allow the vendor to know how much of the material you may order for an upcoming time frame. The time frame can be the next month, week, year, and so on. Generally, the data in this schedule is approximate and the time frame less specific. You will provide the actual dates and quantities in a JIT delivery schedule. The JIT delivery schedule is another form of scheduling agreement release. For example, you need 50 barrels of crude oil on March 31 and 80 barrels on May 16. If you use the supplier workplace, you can make scheduling agreement releases available to your vendors through the Internet.

162. Define FRC and JIT.

- There are two types of scheduling agreement release which are as follows:
  - □ *Forecast (FRC)*—The FRC is a type of scheduling agreement release that you can use with the FRC delivery schedules to provide a medium-term overview of your requirements.

☐ *Just-in-time (JIT)*—JIT delivery is also a type of scheduling agreement release that you can use to schedule and inform your vendor of your requirements in the near future. Such schedules may include daily or even hourly changes in your requirements for the coming few days or weeks.

163. Define "firm zone" and "trade-off zone."

■ When we issue delivery schedules against the scheduling agreements, these delivery schedules are separated into certain time zones. These time zones represent the degree to which the lines of the schedule are binding. Firm zones and trade-off zones are the time zones of delivery schedules. The delivery of these time zones can be understood as follows:

☐ *Firm zone*—This is zone 1, which represents to go ahead with production. The schedule lines of this time zone are calculated as firm. If you cancel the schedule line that falls within the firm zone, you must pay the production costs and cost of procuring input materials to the vendor.

☐ *Trade-off zone*—This is zone 2, which represents to go ahead with procurement of the input materials. This zone is also called the semi-firm zone. The schedule lines of this time zone allow the vendor to take another step toward procuring the required input materials to manufacture the items. Here, items represent the materials that the vendor has to supply. If you cancel the schedule line that falls within the trade-off zone, you must pay the material cost incurred by the vendor.

164. Define "creation profile."

■ A creation profile is a document containing the following information:

☐ Name of the event responsible for creation of a scheduling agreement release.

☐ Method to show the delivery dates.

☐ Whether information about backlogs and immediate requirements are calculated and whether these requirements are part of the scheduling agreement release.

☐ Whether the tolerance check is carried out for scheduling agreement releases. The tolerance check is carried out if the changes are made in the whole delivery system.

165. What does the document type control? How are purchase requisition document types linked with PO and RFQ document types?

■ After indentifying the purchase requirements, the purchasing department converts the purchase requisition into the PO. The SAP R/3 system supports the creation of RFQs that in turn help determine the source to procure purchase requisitions.

■ Now, you create the RFQ for the required materials and send it to chosen vendors. You select the vendors from the vendor master data in your SAP system. These vendors send their quotations. You single out the most favorable quotations by comparing various quotations. Finally, you create a formal PO for the supply of materials or services with the conditions specified in the quotations.

■ This whole process can be understood with the help of Figure 4.3:

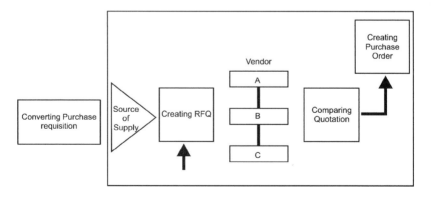

Figure 4.3: Linking of Purchase Requisition Document Types with PO and RFQ Document Types

166. What is tax code?

- Tax code defines how the taxes will be calculated and posted in an SAP R/3 system. Each item to which tax is applicable is allocated a tax code. The SAP R/3 system reads this tax code for each item and calculates the tax for it. This tax and tax code is a part of the PO.

CHAPTER 5
MATERIALS
REQUIREMENT
PLANNING

Materials Requirement Planning

1. What is materials requirement planning (MRP) in SAP?

- MRP guarantees the procurement and production of the required quantities of materials on time. MRP helps a company to determine which materials are to be produced and in what quantity they are to be produced.

2. List the types of MRP.

- The three types of MRP are as follows:
  - *Reorder point planning*—In this type of MRP, procurement starts when the existing stock and receipts fall below the reorder point.
  - *Forecast-based planning*—In this type of MRP, the forecast values and future requirements for materials are decided by the forecasting program.
  - *Time-based planning*—In this type of MRP, the date of the planned requirement should match with a known date, such as the date the vendor delivers materials. If the vendor delivers the materials on this date, then you can start the planning procedure from that date.

3. What MRP procedures are available in consumption-based planning (CBP)?

- The following MRP procedures are available in CBP:
  - ☐ Reorder-point materials planning
  - ☐ Forecast-based materials planning
  - ☐ Time-based materials planning

4. What is the MRP list?

- The MRP list is a static list which is the initial working document from which the MRP controller starts working, and it contains the planning results information for a material. You can access the MRP list for an individual item by using the MD05 transaction code. You can also access the MRP list by using the following navigation path: *SAP Menu > Logistics > Materials Management > MRP > MRP > Evaluations > MRP List–Material*.

5. What are the different transaction codes used for different activities in CBP?

- The following transaction codes are used for different activities in CBP:

Transaction Code	Activity
MDBT	Used in total planning in background mode
MD05	Displays the MRP list
MDLD	Prints the MRP list
MD04	Displays current stock/requirements list
MD01	Used in total planning online
MD12	Used to change planned order
MD13	Displays planned order (individual)

Transaction Code	Activity
MD16	Used to access planned order
MD14	Used to convert planned order to purchase requisition
MD15	Used to convert planned order to purchase requisition
MD20	Used to create planning file entry
MD21	Displays planning file entry
MDAB	Used to set up planning file entries
MD03	Used in single-item and single-level planning
MD07	Displays group of current stock/ requirements list
MD11	Creates planned order

6. What is CBP and how can we integrate it?

■ CBP is the past consumption values of stock, which are used to forecast or determine future requirements. The procedure followed in CBP is not the same as the master production schedule. In CBP, neither the planned independent requirements nor the dependent requirements are responsible for triggering the net requirement calculation. Rather, when the stock levels start falling below a predefined reorder point, the net requirement calculation is triggered by using forecast requirements calculated on the basis of past consumption values.

■ The requirements to implement CBP are as follows:

  □ If the forecast requirements are used in MRP, then the consumption pattern should be constant or linear.

  □ The inventory management is up to date and functioning well.

■ CBP is integrated by using the materials management (MM) component. It is accessed from the *SAP Easy Access* screen by selecting *Logistics > Materials Management > Materials Planning > MRP*.

7.   What is the difference between MRP and CBP?

■ MRP and CBP are two types of SAP planning used to determine a product's requirements. When you plan materials using MRP, you need to predict the materials requirement based on sales and operations planning (SOP). When you follow the CBP approach to plan the materials, you need to predict the future demand of the product. This can be done by using the historical demand for materials.

8.   What important values are used to define the reorder point?

■ The following important values are used to define the reorder point:
  □ Safety stock
  □ Replenishment lead time
  □ Average consumption

9.   What is a procurement proposal? What are the types of procurement proposals?

■ Procurement proposals are created by the system and are based on the settings defined by the purchasing department. They help in ascertaining the required materials.
■ The different types of procurement proposals are:
  □ Purchase requisitions—Required for materials that are procured externally
  □ Schedule lines—Required when a material is procured externally and the material has an identifiable source and scheduling agreement
  □ Planned orders—Required for materials that are procured internally

10.   What is reorder point planning?

■ Reorder point planning is calculated based on a comparison between the available MRP stock and the reorder point, where the MRP stock is the total of plant stock and fixed receipts.

- When the available stock starts falling below the reorder point, procurement is triggered. The important terms to define the reorder point are as follows:

    □ *Safety stock*—Safety stock covers both excess material consumption (within the replenishment lead time) and additional requirements that occur during delivery delays. The important parameters to define the reorder point are as follows:

        - Future requirements or past consumption values
        - Production or vendor delivery timelines
        - Achieved service level
        - Forecast error

    □ *Reorder point*—The reorder point is the threshold value for the available stock. When the available stock falls below this level, proposals for procurement need to be generated.

- The two types of reorder point planning are as follows:

    □ *Manual reorder point planning*—In this type of reorder point planning, you must manually define both the reorder level and the safety stock level within the appropriate material master.

    □ *Automatic reorder point planning*—In this type of reorder point planning, the reorder level and the safety stock level determine the integrated forecasting program. The system calculates the reorder level and the safety stock level using past consumption data and forecast data.

11.   How is the automatic purchase order generated using a particular material after creation of a purchase requisition?

- You need to maintain the source list and select the source list indicator record. In the case of more than one source code list, one of the lists is fixed. You then need to run the MRP. As a result, a purchase requisition is generated with the preassigned supply source list. Lastly, the ME59 transaction code is entered for automatic creation of the purchase order from the purchase requisition.

12. What is forecasting in the SAP system?

■ Forecasting is an uncertain process for predicting future needs. Most business decisions, such as decisions for materials requirements, are based on forecasts. While making business decisions, forecasts are continuously needed. The impact of the forecast on actual results is first evaluated and the initial forecasts are updated; the decisions are then modified accordingly.

13. What are the different models for forecasting?

■ The different models for forecasting are as follows:
   □ *Constant model*—In the constant model, you assume that the quantity of the material used is constant. This does not mean that the quantity of material used is the same every month, but that the material usage variation fluctuates little and therefore a constant mean value can be calculated. This kind of forecasting model applies to things like electricity consumption in an office. Typically, the electricity consumption in an office would not differ a great deal from the mean calculated value.

   □ *Trend model*—The trend model is useful in situations where there is a large increase or decrease in the material over a period of time. It may contain areas of movement away from the trend, but the overall movement follows the trend.

   □ *Seasonal model*—The seasonal model is the one that is affected by conditions such as weather, holidays, or vacations. The seasonal model is a pattern that is repetitive in nature for each period. Therefore, an annual seasonal model can contain a cycle 12 periods long, if the periods are months. This kind of model applies to companies that make patio furniture, which would experience a huge demand in May to September, repeating each year.

   □ *Seasonal trend model*—The seasonal trend model is similar to the seasonal model, except that instead of the same pattern being followed each period, the pattern moves further away from the mean value, which can be either positive or negative.

14.   Can the forecast model be selected automatically?

■ The forecast model can be selected automatically by entering the value J in the forecast model field in the material master record, where the value J is used for automatic model selection.

15.   What are the fields in forecast profile creation?

■ The fields used in forecast profile creation are as follows:
  □ Material
  □ Plant
  □ Base unit of measure
  □ Last forecast
  □ RefMail consumption
  □ Date to
  □ Forecast model
  □ Period indicator
  □ Fiscal year variant
  □ RefPlant consumption
  □ Multiplier
  □ Historical periods
  □ Initialization periods
  □ Forecast periods
  □ Fixed periods
  □ Periods per season
  □ Initialization
  □ Model selection
  □ Optimization level
  □ Alpha factor

- ☐ Gamma factor
- ☐ Tracking limit
- ☐ Selection procedure
- ☐ Weighting group
- ☐ Beta factor
- ☐ Delta factor
- ☐ Reset automatically
- ☐ Parameter optimization
- ☐ Correction factors

16.   What is forecast-based planning?

- Forecast-based planning is a process used in CBP which depends on predictions of future requirements calculated on the basis of the forecast.

17.   What are the different types of forecast model?

- The different types of forecast model are as follows:
  - ☐ Constant
  - ☐ Trend
  - ☐ Seasonal
  - ☐ Seasonal trend

18.   Define "time-phased planning."

- Time-phased planning is an MRP procedure in which materials are delivered at a particular time interval. In time-phased planning, there is a planning file that contains an MRP date to plan the delivery of materials. When the material master is created and is reset for each running plan, the MRP date is also set. If you need to plan the delivery of a material earlier than the specified MRP date, you can enter an MRP date while running the plan. For example, if the running plan is set to Wednesday, you can forward it to Monday.

19. Define "planning process flow."

■ Planning process flow describes the business process and technical system process that are involved in CBP. The system accomplishes the following partial processes in the planning run:

☐ The system first checks the planning file entries and also checks whether or not the material is changed in the planning run.

☐ The system accomplishes a net requirement calculation for every material. It checks whether or not the requirement quantity is covered by available warehouse stock.

☐ After carrying out a net requirement calculation for every material, the system then carries out the log-sizing calculation.

☐ The scheduling is done for the start and finish dates of the procurement proposals.

☐ The system determines the type of procurement proposals and creates planned orders, purchase requisitions, or schedule lines for the materials.

☐ The system creates exception messages and accomplishes a rescheduling check to recognize critical situations, which have to be processed manually in the planning results.

☐ The system also computes the actual days' supply and the receipt days' supply of the materials.

20. Define "planning run type."

■ The planning run type is used to determine materials that are to be planned for sales. Two kinds of planning run type are as follows:

☐ *Net change planning (NETCH)*—In this planning run type, only those materials that have undergone changes relevant to MRP are planned by the system at the time of the last planning run. In other words, in this type only those materials for which the net change planning indicator is set as a planning file entry are planned. When a change has been made in the material that is relevant to MRP, the system sets the planning indicator.

- Changes that cause an entry in the planning file are as follows:
- Changes to the stock
- Changes in the creation of purchase requisitions, purchase orders, sales requirements, forecast requirements, planned orders, and dependent requirements
- Changes in the fields that are related to the planning run
- Changes in the deletion receipt or issue quantities
  - □ *Regenerative planning (NEUPL)*—In this planning run type, the system plans all materials contained in the planning file.

21. Define "planning calendars."

- Planning calendars outline flexible period lengths for MRP at the plant level. They are used to define period totals in the stock/requirements list and flexible splitting periods for demand management.

22. How can we create a planning calendar in CBP?

- You can create a planning calendar by using the MD25 transaction code or by using the following path: *SAP Menu > Logistics > Material Management > MRP > MRP > Master Data > Planning Calendar > Create Periods.*

23. How is planning done at the plant level and storage location level?

- Planning is done at two levels:
  - □ *Plant level*—This is the base level of planning.
  - □ *Storage location level*—The plant level takes all the storage locations into consideration while planning. However, there might be a case when the client may not want to plan at that level.

- At the plant level, planning is done by performing the following steps:

  □ The system checks the entries in the planning file. This involves checking the materials which have been changed and then deciding if the materials need to be included in the planning process.

  □ The available warehouse stock is checked to ensure that the quantity that is required is available. If the quantity is less than the required amount, a procurement proposal is created.

  □ A bulk calculation is then performed.

  □ A schedule is made to choose the start and end dates of the procurement proposals.

  □ You can also assign a supplier, if required.

  □ There can be critical situations that are identified using exception messages. In such situations, you need to perform the whole process manually.

  □ The actual days taken for supply and receipt of the product are calculated.

- For planning at the storage location level, there are two options:

  □ *Planning at the storage location level*—The planning department has to make sure that the reorder level and the replacement quantities are defined at the storage location level.

  □ *Excluding the storage location from planning*—The planning department can also exclude the storage location from planning by selecting an appropriate value for the MRP.

24. How is the net requirement calculated?

- The net requirement calculation is used to determine uncovered product requirements during procurement planning for a location product. The system has the product requirements consumed, the product stock, the existing production planning (PP), and supply network planning (SNP) product receipts needed to perform the net requirement calculation. The net requirements calculation is done by using the following process flow:

- ☐ The system first computes plant stock. For all storage locations belonging to a specified plant and not excluded from materials planning or planned separately, the stocks grouped together to constitute the entire plant stock are as follows:
  - Unrestricted-use stock
  - Stock in quality inspection
  - Unrestricted-use consignment stock
  - Consignment warehouse stock in quality inspection
- ☐ The system also knows all the goods issues and receipts for a material. Some examples of a goods issue are customer requirements, planned independent requirements, and reservations, and some examples of receipts are planned orders and purchase requisitions.
- ☐ The system verifies that the requirement is covered for every issue date. If the requirement against each issue date is not covered, then the system calculates the shortage in quantity of materials and creates a procurement proposal.

- Types of planning supported by the net requirement calculation are as follows:
  - ☐ Reorder point planning
  - ☐ Forecast-based planning
  - ☐ MRP

25. How is the lot-size calculation performed in MRP?

- The lot-size calculation is performed in MRP to get the quantity of material to be produced or procured. It is done in the SAP system by comparing the value of the shortage quantity with the chosen value of the parameter of the lot-sizing procedure. In addition, if a rounding value or a rounding profile is specified, then the SAP system rounds up the lot size and then calculates the procurement quantity.

■ The lot-size calculation is required when the system determines that there are material shortages for any requirement date. These shortage quantities are shown by receipt elements. The system then calculates the quantities required for the receipts in the planning run in the procurement quantity calculation.

26.   What are static lot-sizing procedures?

■ Static lot-sizing procedures are used to calculate the procurement quantity with the help of quantity specifications, which are entered in the material master. The different types of static lot-sizing procedures are as follows:

   ☐ Lot-for-log order quantity

   ☐ Fixed-lot size

   ☐ Fixed-lot size with splitting and overlapping

   ☐ Replenishment up to maximum stock level

27.   What is a rounding profile?

■ A rounding profile is used to adjust the order proposal quantity for deliverable units in the planning run. It is used when the procurement quantity is to be rounded up to quantities that can be delivered. A rounding profile contains a threshold as well as rounding values. If the requirement is below the first threshold value, then the system copies the original requirement value, which is left unchanged. However, if the requirement is above the first threshold value, the system always rounds up the requirement value.

28.   How is scheduling carried out in MRP?

■ When the system has calculated the quantity that is to be procured in the lot-size calculation, the scheduling is carried out in MRP. Scheduling is used to determine the order start date and the order finish date of the procurement elements. The following requirements are needed to schedule the external procurement:

☐ You must define the processing time for purchasing in work days either with customized MRP, in the plant parameters, or in the work step.

☐ You must define the planned delivery time of the material in calendar days, which must be maintained in the material master record.

☐ You must define the goods receipt processing time in work days in the material master record.

29. What is the difference between backward scheduling and forward scheduling?

■ The process of scheduling an order in the forward direction, that is, from the project's estimated start date to the end date, is known as forward scheduling. You use this scheduling to calculate the project's start and end dates.

■ The process of scheduling an order in the backward direction, that is, from the end date to the start date, is known as backward scheduling.

30. What are the basic types of model selection?

■ The following are the three basic types of model selection:

☐ Manual model selection

☐ Automatic model selection

☐ Manual model selection with additional system check

31. How is the procurement type determined?

■ To determine the procurement type, you need to enter procurement type F for the material planned by using CBP. You can also enter procurement type X in the material master record for in-house production. You can then determine the procurement type by using the following process:

- ☐ Overwriting the indicator in the material master record
- ☐ Converting the planned order either by using a production order or by using a purchase requisition
- ☐ Defining quotas for external procurement and in-house production in the quota file

32.   What is the use of the special procurement type?

- ■ The special procurement type is used to define how procurement is to be accomplished in CBP. For this, you need to define the special procurement type for stock transfer from plant to plant. The methods of special procurement for in-house production are as follows:
    - ☐ Withdrawal from an alternative plant
    - ☐ Phantom assemblies
    - ☐ Production in alternative plant
    - ☐ Direct production
- ■ The methods of special procurement for external procurement are as follows:
    - ☐ Subcontracting
    - ☐ Stock transfer
    - ☐ Consignment

33.   How does the system automatically determine the source of supply?

- ■ When purchase requisitions or delivery schedules are created during the planning run, the system determines the source of supply directly from the planning procedure. You can determine the source of supply by using the following method:
    - ☐ Determining the source of supply by using the source list
        - ■ In this method, the system first checks whether a quota arrangement is maintained for the materials.

The system then checks if only one entry exists in the source list, which is similar to materials requirement planning. The indicator for the source list must be set for a particular vendor so that the system can create purchase requisitions and delivery schedules during the planning run and automatically assign them to the vendor. You must also maintain a scheduling agreement for a delivery schedule.

- When you properly maintain all the entries, the system creates a purchase requisition with the source of the supply, and this is recorded in the source list.

☐ Determining the source of supply by using quota arrangements and source lists

- In this method, the system first checks whether a quota arrangement is valid for the delivery date of the purchase requisitions, which is maintained in the quota file for the material.

- The system then checks whether the indicator for quota arrangement is correctly maintained in the material master. The system then finds out from which vendor the material should be procured by using the quotas specified for the vendors.

- Next, the system checks whether an entry for the vendor, which exists in the source list, is relevant to MRP.

- To maintain the source list, select *Master Data > Source List > Maintain Option* from the *Purchasing Task* menu.

34. What is meant by the term "confirmation control key"?

- The confirmation control key is used to control the process of creating the purchase order. In the purchase order, the confirmation control key has the following functions:

  ☐ The confirmation control key regulates whether the confirmations are relevant for goods receipt or material planning and whether confirmations are expected for a specific purchase order.

☐ When the goods receipt posting for the inbound delivery is carried out and you want to create a material document, then the goods receipt assignment must be defined in the confirmation control key.

■ You can navigate the following menu path to configure the confirmation control key: *SPRO > MM > Purchasing > Confirmations > Set Up Confirmation Control*

■ The transaction code of the confirmation control key is OMGZ

35.   What is the MRP area?

■ The MRP area is an organizational unit used to determine which MRP is to be carried out independently outside the total plant-level MRP run. The three types of MRP areas are as follows:

☐ *Plant MRP area*—Consists of the plant with all its storage locations and stock

☐ *MRP areas for storage locations*—Consists of a particular storage location, which creates an MRP area and assigns the storage location to the MRP area

☐ *MRP areas for subcontractors*—Consists of a subcontractor, who assigns only one MRP area

36.   What are the control parameters for planning runs?

■ Control parameters are used for total planning procedures and for single-item planning; they can be set in the initial screen of the planning run. They are also used to determine how the planning run is executed and which results are produced. The control parameters used for planning runs are as follows:

☐ *Planning run type*—In this control parameter, you can select all materials that need to be planned or only those materials whose MRP has changed.

☐ *Planning mode*—In this control parameter, you can ascertain how the system deals with procurement proposals.

☐ *Scheduling*—In this control parameter, you can select the base date calculation or lead-time scheduling.

37. Define "creation indicators."

■ Creation indicators are part of the process of creating purchase requisitions, schedule lines, and MRP list indicators. They define whether or not the planned orders, purchase requisitions, or schedule lines are to be created externally for materials procured. They also define whether or not MRP lists are created. Different types of creation indicators are as follows:

□ *Creation indicator for purchase requisitions*—Determines whether or not purchase requisitions that are to be created for materials are procured externally. When you use this indicator, the system creates purchase requisitions instead of a planned order. The following options are available to create indicators for purchase requisitions:

  ■ Only planned orders

  ■ Only purchase requisitions

  ■ Purchase requisitions within the opening period

  ■ Planned orders outside the opening period

□ *Creation indicator for schedule lines*—Determines whether or not schedule lines are created directly and materials are procured externally. Options that exist in the creation indicator for schedule lines are as follows:

  ■ Only schedule lines

  ■ No schedule lines

  ■ Schedule lines within the opening period

  ■ Purchase requisitions outside the opening period

□ *Creation indicator for MRP lists*—Determines whether the result of the planning run is stored in the form of MRP lists. These MRP lists are executed after the planning run. Options that exist in the creation indicator for MRP lists are as follows:

  ■ No MRP lists

  ■ Always MRP lists

  ■ MRP lists with certain exceptional situations documented in exception messages

38.   What are the conditions required to create the planned orders?

■   The system must create an internal procurement proposal; then, planned orders are created. In the case of vendor procurement, a planned order is created by the MRP controller.

39.   What is the transaction code to convert planned orders into purchase requisitions?

■   MD14 is the transaction code to convert planned orders into purchase requisitions.

40.   What is total planning?

■   The planning of all materials that are related to requirement planning is known as total planning. It includes the bill of material (BOM) explosion for the materials. Total planning can be used for a single plant, or it can be used to control the total planning run for multiple plants. Total planning can be used in the following areas:

  ☐   Several plant areas
  ☐   One MRP area
  ☐   Several MRP areas
  ☐   A combination of plants and MRP areas

41.   How is the procurement proposal created through MRP?

■   During the planning run, the system automatically creates procurement proposals. Procurement proposals determine when inward stock movement should be made and when the quantity of stock is expected in MRP. It includes the following tasks:

☐ Planned orders

☐ Purchase requisitions

☐ Schedule lines

■ The following conversions require additional components:

☐ The materials master (LO-MD-MM) component is required to convert the planned orders.

☐ The production orders (PP-SFC) and routing (PP-BD-RTG) components are required to convert planned orders into production orders.

☐ The production planning for process industries (PP-PI) component is required to convert planned orders into process orders.

☐ The purchasing (MM-PUR) component is required to convert purchase requisitions into purchase orders.

☐ The capacity planning (PP-CRP) component is required to execute capacity leveling.

42. Define "planned order." How is it created?

■ A planned order is sent to a plant for the procurement of a particular material at a given time. It determines when the inward material movement should be made in MRP. The characteristics of a planned order are as follows:

☐ Planned orders can be changed or deleted at any time, except that planned orders for direct production and for direct procurement cannot be changed or deleted at any time.

☐ They do not bind and do not trigger procurement directly.

☐ They specify the basic dates for in-house production of material.

■ The following two methods are used to create planned orders:

☐ *Automatic creation of planned orders*—In this method of creating a planned order, the system automatically calculates the materials, requirement quantity, and date on which the material is to be procured. The system then creates the corresponding planned order and also calculates the BOM that is produced in-house and uses the BOM to create a planned order.

- □ *Manual creation of planned orders*—In this method, you create planned orders manually. To do this, you have to determine which materials need to be procured, whether materials are to be procured externally or internally, the quantities of materials that are to be procured, and on which date the materials are available for the planned order.

43. How is a planned order converted into a purchase requisition?

- ■ The following steps are followed to convert a planned order into a purchase requisition:
  - □ Select the MRP node and then select *Planned Order > Convert to Purchase Requisition > Individual Conversion*. The individual conversion of planned orders screen appears.
  - □ Enter the number of planned orders to be converted into purchase requisitions and select ✅. A detailed screen appears displaying the individual conversion of planned orders.
- ■ The first part of the screen contains the planned order data and the second part displays the purchase requisition data. As seen, the data is drawn partly from the planned order and partly from the material master. If required, you can overwrite this data.
  - □ Enter the data as needed.
  - □ Change the converted quantity field value to the quantity that is actually converted and transferred to the purchase requisition, and then press the Enter key.
  - □ Save all the entries or values entered in the individual conversion of planned orders screen.

44. Define "planning time fence."

■ The planning time fence protects the master plan from automatic changes in the master plan items. The system does not create or update the order proposals for the planning time fence during the planning run. It dynamically calculates the end date of the planning time fence beginning from the planning date. The planning time fence is used for materials planned in MRP, master schedule items in master production scheduling, and materials in long-term planning.

45. How can we disable a reservation in MRP?

■ You can disable a reservation in MRP by using the transaction code OPPI. This is also used to check the blocked stock.

CHAPTER 6
INVENTORY
MANAGEMENT

Inventory Management

1. Give an overview of inventory management in the SAP system.

■ Inventory management in the SAP system helps record and track stocks of materials. It also involves the planning and documentation of all goods movements.

2. What tasks are covered under inventory management?

■ Inventory management is an important part of materials management (MM). Optimal inventory management not only ensures an uninterrupted supply of the material at the required time, but also prevents wasting items. MM covers the following tasks:
  □ Material stock management
  □ Planning, entry, and documentation of goods transfers from and to the inventory
  □ Physical stocking of items

3. What is physical inventory?

■ Physical inventory is a process in which all the transactions related to the movement of goods are stopped and the company physically counts inventory. It is required in financial accounting rules or for placing an accurate value on the inventory for tax purposes.

4. What are the initial configuration steps for purchase acquisition?

- The steps for purchase acquisition are as follows:
  - ☐ Defining the default values for the physical inventory document
  - ☐ Reporting batch inputs
  - ☐ Recording tolerances for physical inventory differences
  - ☐ Inventory sampling as well as configuration of cycle counting

5. What is the difference between managing stock by quantity and managing stock by value?

- Transactions that make changes in the stock result in stock updates that are recorded in real time. At any point in time one can view the stock overview, which represents the current situation at that time. That is the essence of stock management by quantity, and can applied to the following stock types:
  - ☐ Located in the warehouse
  - ☐ Ordered but not yet received
  - ☐ Located in the warehouse and reserved for a particular purpose
  - ☐ Reserved for quality inspection
- The managing stock by value option reviews the stock materials qualitatively rather than quantitatively. The valuation of stock is done either at the plant level or at the location level. Updates that can be done when managing stock by value are as follows:

□ The quantity and value for the goods movement

□ The accounts that are assigned for cost accounting

□ The G/L accounts for financial accounts, with automatic assignment of accounts

■ The valuation area is the organizational level at which the stock value is maintained. It can be either at plant level or storage level.

6.   What are "special stocks" in SAP?

■ Special stocks are defined as stocks that must be managed separately by a company. They can be either company-owned or external stocks. They can be categorized as follows:

□ Consignment

□ Subcontracting

□ Stock transfer using stock transport order

□ Third-party processing

□ Returnable transport packaging

□ Pipeline handling

□ Sales-order stock

□ Project stock

7.   With which modules in SAP is inventory management integrated?

■ Inventory management is an important part of the SAP MM module. The business activities of an organization revolve around the inventory of materials, which serves as the input for the manufacturing process or the inventory of prepared goods for delivery or sale. The material is purchased from the appropriate vendors on the basis of requests from the materials requirement planning (MRP) module. The delivered items are recorded as the goods receipt in inventory management. The materials are then stored, either for delivery to the customer or for manufacturing processes. Inventory management is integrated with other modules, such as financial accounting (FI), sales and distribution (SD), production planning (PP), project system (PS), and quality management (QM).

8. How is inventory management integrated with the MM module?

■ Inventory management is directly linked with the MM module because any movement of goods to and from inventory happens under the MM module. MRP, purchasing, and invoice verification are some of the MM components that are also linked with inventory management. After material is ordered it is posted as a goods receipt with reference to the purchase order. The actual data of the quantities are checked in the vendor's invoice.

9. What are the initial configuration steps for inventory management?

■ The steps for inventory management are as follows:
  □ Defining plant parameters
  □ Defining system message attributes
  □ Defining number assignment
  □ Defining goods issue, transfer posting, screen layout
  □ Maintaining copy rules for reference documents
  □ Setting up dynamic availability checks
  □ Confirming the negative items

10. What is "goods movement"? What types of documents are created after goods movement?

■ Goods movement refers to the movement of stock. This movement of stock could be either inbound from the vendor, outbound to a customer, between different plants, or even between different stocks within a plant. After goods movement, the SAP system creates two types of documents: material documents and accounting documents.

11. What are the goods movements that take place in the MM module?

■ The goods movements can be defined as the physical or logical movements of materials that lead to a change in stock levels or results in material consumption. The goods movements are part of the MM policy. The goods movements in SAP are as follows:

  □ *Goods receipt*—Represents the physical movement of goods or materials into the company. It increases the stock quantity. The goods receipt can be of the following types:

    ▪ Goods receipt with reference to a purchase order

    ▪ Goods receipt with reference to a production order

    ▪ Goods receipt without reference

  □ *Goods issue*—Represents the physical movement of goods or material out of the company. It reduces the stock quantity. The goods issue can be of the following types:

    ▪ Goods consumption in the company

    ▪ Goods delivery to customers

  □ *Stock transfer*—Represents the movement of materials from one location to another location. The locations can be either within the same plant or different plants.

  □ *Transfer posting*—Represents the stock transfer that can either be physical or logical. In logical stock transfers, goods are transferred only in records, while the actual stock transfer does not occur. Some examples of physical stock transfer are:

    ▪ Stock transfer between two storage locations in a plant

    ▪ Stock transfer between two plants

    ▪ Transfer of materials to customer consignment stock

■ Some examples of logical stock transfer are:
  □ Release of materials from stock in quality inspection
  □ Transfer of materials from vendor consignment stock to own stock
  □ Batch splitting
  □ Transfer posting material-to-material

12. What are "goods receipt" and "goods issue"?

■ Goods receipt is the process that enables the receipt of material from a vendor or from the in-house production process. There are other types of goods receipts in SAP that include initial stock creation. The goods receipt process also increases stock due to one of the following processes:
  □ Receipt of production order
  □ Receipt of purchase order
  □ Initial inventory entry
  □ Others
■ Goods issue is a process in which the stock in the warehouse is reduced due to any of the following reasons:
  □ Shipment to a customer
  □ Stock withdrawal for a production order
  □ Return of materials
  □ Material required for sampling
  □ Scrapping of materials

13. Why is goods receipt important to a company?

■ Goods receipt indicates a receipt or inward movement of stock of materials or goods. When an external vendor provides stock to the company, the goods receipt is generated as a purchase order, and when the material is produced in-house, the goods receipt is generated as a production order. A goods receipt is important to a company because using a goods receipt moves material into stock, updates the stock levels, and thereby indirectly enables the production process.

14.   How is a goods receipt performed?

- The steps to perform a goods receipt are as follows:
    - ☐ Enter the header data.
    - ☐ Select the movement type and the purchase order number.
- The document is posted in the database.

15.   How do you post the goods if the purchase order number is not known?

- If the purchase order number is not known, you must enter search criteria for the purchase order in the initial screen. As a result, the list of purchase orders is displayed. The desired purchase order items can then be copied.

16.   How is the vendor return processed without a purchase order reference?

- You first need to observe the Return column and then select *Item Detail > MIGO_GR > Goods Receipt for Purchase Order*. If the intention is to deduct the stock, then movement type 161 is used; otherwise, 162 is used to undo the changes. Lastly, you must ensure that the document is a return purchase order. The document is then saved.
- Alternatively, you can use the M21N transaction code for this purpose.

17.   What happens when a goods receipt is posted?

- While posting a goods receipt, the following events occur:
    - ☐ The material document is created.
    - ☐ The accounting document is created.
    - ☐ Three printed versions of goods receipt notes are modified.
    - ☐ The stock level changes.

18.   What are the types of goods receipts that cannot be received through normal procedures? How do we receive these goods?

- The following types of goods receipts cannot be received through normal procedures:
  - Goods receipts without production orders
  - Goods receipts of by-products
  - Goods receipts for free goods
- The processes for receiving these goods are as follows:
- Goods receipts without production orders:
  - If SAP PP is not implemented in the company, then the goods receipts of finished goods from production cannot reference a production order. In such a case, the material is received into the stock using a miscellaneous goods receipt. Goods receipts without production orders can be accessed through the transaction code MB1C or by following the navigation path: *SAP Menu > Logistics > Materials Management > Inventory Management > Goods Receipt > Other*. Goods receipts for finished goods without production orders also require any of the following movement types:
    - 521—Goods receipts for finished goods without production orders into unrestricted stock
    - 523—Goods receipts for finished goods without production orders into quality inspection stock
    - 525—Goods receipts for finished goods without production orders into blocked stock
- Goods receipts of by-products:
  - In the case of goods receipts of by-products, the company receives the materials into stock using the MB1C transaction code with movement type 531, which is used only for receiving by-products.
- Goods receipts for free goods:
  - In the case of goods receipts for free goods, the company receives the materials into stock using the MB1C transaction code along with movement type 511, which is used for receiving these types of goods.

19. How can a goods receipt be posted when the purchase order number is unknown?

■ If the goods receipt does not have a purchase order, some companies do not accept the goods receipt and refuse to accept the delivery. Other companies accept the delivery of materials and keep the materials in the quality or blocked stock until the situation is resolved. To obtain the goods receipt without a purchase order number, these companies use the MIGO transaction. After entering the required details for the material, the goods receipt is posted and the material becomes a part of the plant stock.

20. What are the results of goods movements?

■ The following events are initiated when goods movements take place:
  □ First, a materials document is generated, which is proof of the goods movements.
  □ Accounting documents are generated if the movement of goods requires a change in the financial accounts.
  □ The stocks of the materials quantities are updated.
  □ The stock values in the material master are updated.
  □ Financial and material documents are updated.

21. How do we receive goods from production?

■ Goods from production can be posted either to the warehouse or consumption. They are posted with the same movement type.

22. What documents are created with goods movement?

■ Proper documentation is a part of maintaining authentication over the business process. The proper documents must be generated and prepared for every transaction affecting the material stock, including goods movement.

In the case of goods movements, the following documents are prepared:

☐ *Material documents*—This is the document that is generated when the goods movement is posted. It is proof of the movement of goods. The material document contains general data relating the movement of the goods and items.

☐ *Accounting documents*—Accounting documents are prepared if the goods movements influence the financial accounting. They are prepared parallel to the material documents. Apart from the preceding documents, there are a number of documents that are prepared alongside the material documents associated with goods movements. The G/L accounts associated with a goods movement are updated through an automatic goods assignment.

■ Accounting entries contain local as well as foreign currencies. This is so that the goods movements are automatically managed in the context of both the local and foreign currencies.

23. How is a material document cancelled?

■ A material document is cancelled when you specify the wrong entries, such as the wrong material quantity and goods movements, during the creation of the material document.

☐ Cancelling goods movements requires the following:

☐ *Entering a reverse document*—A reverse document is entered with a reference to the original document. The advantage of this is that the cancelled documents are copied from the original documents. The reversal of goods issued, transfer posting, and goods receipts without references are posted with the value of the original documents. The reversal of goods with reference to the purchase order or production order is posted with the values specified in the purchase order or production order.

☐ *Entering a material document*—A reverse document is entered with a reference to the material document. Here, the material documents are entered with the reversal movement type. In this case, no reference is made to any document, but all the data are entered manually.

■ Since there is no reference to the material document, the system re-determines the values of the posting. In the case of any change in the price of the material, the new price of the materials is used.

24.   How can we find the logical value of stock items?

■ You can use the MC49 transaction code to find the logical value of stock items by date.

25.   What are the ways of receiving goods?

■ Goods can be received per the reference to inbound delivery. Different ways of receiving the goods are as follows:

  □ Order
  □ Others
  □ Outbound delivery
  □ Purchase order
  □ Reservation
  □ Transport
  □ Transport ID code

26.   What is the movement type?

■ While implementing goods movements in an organization, you must enter the movement type, which is a three-digit identification key. The following are the common movement types that are used in SAP:

  □ 102—Goods that are received against a purchase order
  □ 201—Goods that are issued
  □ 321—Goods released from quality inspection stock

27.   What does a movement type control?

■ The movement type acts as a controlling factor in inventory management. It controls the following activities:

  ☐ Updating quantity

  ☐ Updating consumption and stock

  ☐ Displaying particular fields in a document

28.   What is a planned goods receipt?

■ Planned documents contain data for future procurements such as goods receipts, purchase orders, and others. There are three planned goods receipts:

  ☐ *Using purchase orders*—If purchase components are used to purchase the materials from the vendor, then there is no need for the manual planning of a goods receipt. Here, the purchase order created by MM purchasing contains all the information required for the goods receipt.

  ☐ *Using production orders*—If the goods receipt is planned using the production order, then there is no need for the manual planning of a goods receipt from the production, since the order contains all of the information regarding the purchase.

  ☐ *Using reservations*—If the MM component or purchase order is not present, this type is used. In this case, the reservations of the planned goods receipt from the vendor or production need to be entered.

29.   What is goods receipt blocked stock? How is a material received in goods also received in blocked stock?

■ Goods receipt blocked stock is the quantity of a material delivered by a vendor that has not yet been placed in final storage.

■ In the case of the receipt of materials in the goods receipt blocked stock, the following activities are performed:

☐ *Preparation of material documents*—The first activity is the preparation of the material documents, which act as a log file for posting and recording the items. In the case of items that are posted in the goods receipt blocked stocks, no accounting posting is done nor any accounting documents created.

☐ *Updating the stock*—In the case of posting for goods receipt blocked stocks, stocks are not updated. The goods received blocked stocks increase the purchase order history.

☐ *Updating the G/L account*—The G/L account is not updated when the goods are received in blocked stock.

☐ *Updating the purchase order*—In the case of posting in goods receipt blocked stock, the open purchase order is not affected.

30. List the movement types for unplanned goods received.

■ The following are the movement types used for unplanned goods received:
  ☐ 501
  ☐ 561
  ☐ 531

31. What are the ways through which we can receive goods without a reference?

■ There are certain instances when goods can be received without a reference. Such cases may be one or all of the following:

  ☐ Transfer of inventory balances from an existing system to a SAP R/3 system.

  ☐ Goods can be received as miscellaneous items if the goods receipt is not formulated by using an MM component.

  ☐ Goods can be be treated as miscellaneous items with a reservation if the goods are received without a production order.

- Goods can be received as a by-product and treated as a miscellaneous item.

- A product that is delivered free of charge is treated as an other receipt.

- Goods that are returned from a customer can be received without a reference.

32. How is a return delivery posted in the sales documents?

- Returning goods that are part of an enterprise stock to a third-party supplier is called a return delivery.
- Depending upon the customization of the sales, the delivery can be posted to the following stocks:
  - *Blocked stock returns*—This stock holds the returned goods, which are not valuated and used without restriction.
  - *Unrestricted-use stock*—This type of stock holds unrestricted goods.
  - *Quality-inspection stock*—This type of stock holds returned goods that are inspected for quality.
  - *Blocked stock*—This type of stock holds returned goods that are blocked.
- If a quantity posted to blocked stock returns first, then a manual posting of the goods movement is done in the inventory management component to transfer the quantity to the valuated stock.

33. How can an item be returned to a vendor?

- While posting the goods to the goods receipt in the purchase order, you need to enter the items that can be returned to the vendor. There is no need to explicitly reference the purchase order.

34. What is goods issue reversal?

- The process of issuing the material back into the stock of material is known as a goods issue reversal. For example, if the goods issued to the production order are 500 kg of material and only 300 kg is consumed, then the remaining 200 kg is returned to stock.

35. What are the documents that are created when a goods issue is posted?

■ The following documents are created when a goods issue is posted:

☐ Material documents

☐ Accounting documents

☐ Goods issue slip

☐ Stock changes

☐ General ledger account changes

36. What are the results of the goods issue?

■ The goods issue is any upward movement of goods that results in the following activities:

☐ *Creation of material documents*—A material document is created from the goods issue as a proof of goods movement.

☐ *Creation of accounting documents*—Accounting documents are created parallel to the material documents and contain postings in the corresponding accounts that are affected by the goods movement.

☐ *Printing of receipt/issue slip*—The goods issued are entered, and you can also print the goods issue slip.

☐ *Stock update*—The stock is updated after the goods are issued. The following types of stock are reduced due to goods issue:

  ▪ Total-valued

  ▪ Unrestricted-use

  ▪ Reservation

The material planning and available stocks remain unchanged while posting for a planned goods issue, since the quantity withdrawn is reserved and not available.

- ☐ *G/L accounts update*—When posting the goods issued, G/L accounts are updated.
- ☐ *Consumption update*—In the case of goods receipts, the consumption statistics of the materials in the material master are updated and reflected in the plant stock availability.
- ☐ *Reservation update*—If the goods issued are referenced by a reservation or sales order, then the quantity is updated in the reservation system. The reservation item is complete when the total quantity is withdrawn.
- ☐ *Updated order*—In the case of goods issued with reference to an order, the quantities issued are updated in the order.
- ☐ *Other applications updates*—There might be a case when some other related applications are updated. For example, after the goods are issued, the cost center field is updated.
- ☐ *Transfer requirement creation*—If the storage locations involved with goods issue are managed by the warehouse management system, then a transfer requirement is created.
- ☐ *Inspection lot creation*—Inspection of the issued material is done in cases when the quality processing system is active.

37.   Where is the goods issue performed?

- ■ The goods issue is performed in the *Goods Issue Purchase Order* screen. You need to select *Goods Issue* and click the initial screen to arrive at the *Goods Issue Purchase Order* screen. Alternatively, you can also use the MIGO transaction code for this purpose.

38.   How can we perform the goods issue in SAP?

- ■ To perform the goods issue, you first need to enter the header data and then select *Goods Issue > Create with Reference > To Order*. You need to enter the order number if it is known.

39. What are goods issues to a production order, to scrap, and for sampling?

■ *Goods issues to a production order*—The MRP process plans the production order. In addition, it ensures that the materials mentioned in the bill of materials are available for the production of the finished goods. Further, it ensures that the MM process supplies materials to the production order with the help of a goods issue.

■ *Goods issues to scrap*—Materials that are no longer of any use or value to the company are known as scrap. Such materials need to be removed from stock. The inventory manager performs the goods issue operation with the movement type relevant to scrap a material.

■ *Goods issue for sampling*—Companies take samples of materials to test for quality. To test a sample material, it needs to be first removed from the stock. The inventory manager performs a goods issue of the materials that need to be sent for sampling.

40. How is a goods issue done in SAP?

■ The goods issue is a broad concept that covers outward movement of goods from the organization. The following instances of goods movement are considered goods issues:

☐ Transfer of stock for production

☐ Samples withdrawn

☐ Goods returned to the vendors

☐ Delivery to customer

☐ Material issued for other purposes such as for cost centers or maintenance

■ Each type of goods issue is handled in SAP R/3 MM in the following ways:

☐ If the materials are withdrawn for the production order, they are treated as goods issued with reference to the production order.

☐ If the goods are returned to the vendors, then this is entered in the function material document.

☐ If the goods are scrapped, this is entered as a goods issue.

41. How is a material scrapped?

■ The scrapping of material is a process to withdraw goods or materials that are no longer used. It is a normal part of replenishing stock. The following types of material stocks are eligible for scrapping:

  □ Unrestricted-used stock

  □ Quality-inspected stock

  □ Blocked stock

■ The results of scrapping of materials can be:

  □ Reduction of relevant stock

  □ Posting of the figures of scrapped materials from stock account to scrapped account

  □ Assignment of the cost of the scrapped material to specific cost centers

42. What is availability check?

■ The availability check is the stock check that the system runs automatically when a goods movement occurs in the organization. It prevents negative inventory balances of the physical stock categories (such as unrestricted-use stock).

■ The resulting data is used for various purposes ranging from planning to allocation. The following are different types of availability checks done in the SAP MM module:

  □ *Availability check for different types of stock in inventory management*—For each type of materials movement, the availability check is automatically carried out in the system to prevent the reading of the physical stock from being negative. The system checks the availability of each of the items in the stocks and determines if the desired quantity can be withdrawn. For example, if the unrestricted stock is checked in this case and it is found that withdrawal is not permissible, then an error message is generated. The availability check for the stock in question is done at the plant level, storage location, and special stock level.

- *Availability of stocks in materials*—This type of availability check is done in the context of materials planning to prevent reissuing of an already reserved item.

43.   How do we create a return delivery to the vendor?

- There are some circumstances, such as poor quality or damaged items, when goods are returned to the vendors. If a substitute delivery is sent by the vendor, then posting of this goods receipt is done in the reference of the returned delivery.

  - *Return delivery by shipping*—The goods returned can be posted by shipping. The goods can be returned from the following stocks in the case of return delivery by shipping:

    - Unrestricted-use
    - Quality inspection
    - Blocked
    - Goods receipt blocked stocks

  - *Prerequisites*—Before entering a return delivery, the purchase order and material documents must be referenced. This is necessary for some system-generated suggestions, such as storage location, matching of the returned or ordered quantities, and reduction of the delivery date. This is also necessary to return the stock to the same stock from where it was supplied.

- *Activities*—The following activities are related to the return delivery of the documents:

  - *Posting a return delivery by referring to the material document*—In the case of goods returned to the vendors by shipping, the number and year of the material document are entered. Next, the delivery note number and vendor fields are entered.

  - *Posting a return delivery by referring to the purchase order*—In the case of goods returned to the vendors with reference to the purchase order, the goods movements to purchase order or goods receipt are entered.

□ *Posting a goods receipt by referring to a return delivery*—You must reference the return delivery while posting for substitute goods receipt after the delivery is returned to the vendor. The proper verification of the invoice related to the goods receipt should also be made so that the returned delivery and invoice remain correct. The reversal movement types used to reference the associated return delivery can be shown as:

Goods receipt	Return delivery	Substitute delivery
101	122	123
103	124	125
105	122	123

44. What is a stock transfer?

■ Stock transfer is the transfer of materials from one place of storage to another place of storage.

■ You can transfer stock in a single plant or between two different plants. This is usually done per planning policies and business expansions. Types of movements of the internal stocks in an organization during a stock transfer are as follows:

□ *Company code to company code*—This is the transfer of stocks from one complete business unit to another. This can be done either inside or outside the organization.

□ *Plant to plant*—Stocks can be transferred from one plant to another plant due to internal materials planning or administrative reasons. This kind of stock transfer usually takes place from the unrestricted stock of one plant to another.

□ *Storage location to storage location*—In this category, the transfer is done from one storage location to another within a plant. As a result, the stock quantities at both locations need to be updated.

■ The different procedures to carry out a stock transfer are as follows:

□ *One-step procedure*—In this procedure, only one transaction is entered into the system as the stock transfer moves the stock from an issuing point to a receiving point.

☐ *Two-step procedure*—The stock is monitored during transit. After the goods issue is posted at the issuing point, the stock appears at the receiving point and is managed in that system as well.

☐ *Stock transport order*—In the case of stock transfer using stock transport orders, the following modules are involved:

- Purchasing
- Inventory management
- Invoice verification
- Billing

■ Stock transfer using stock transport orders can be done without delivery documents, with delivery documents, or with delivery as well as billing documents. The following are the advantages of the stock transport order:

☐ Planned goods receipt

☐ Entering of vendor in the stock transport order

☐ Entering of delivery cost in the stock transport order

☐ Conversion of the purchase order (or the purchase requisition in the purchase order).

☐ Running the availability check for the stock transfer

45.   What are the different ways of making a stock transfer?

■ A stock transfer can be made physically or logically. In other words, when you move material from one storage location to another, the stock transfer was done physically. When you move stock from quality inspection status to unrestricted status, the stock transfer was done logically.

46.   What is a transfer posting?

■ Physical and logical stock transfers are collectively called the transfer posting. Stock transfers typically change the stock type, batch number, or material number. The transfer posting is related to the documentation of the stock changes resulting from a stock transfer.

47. How is stock transferred from one storage location to another?

- Stock transfer from one storage location to another is carried out within a plant. The posting of this kind of transfer is done without entering the value of the stock materials, as the management of the items is done within the same plant.

48. How is stock transferred from one plant to another plant?

- The transfer of the stock from one plant to another is a bigger activity compared to transfers done within the same plant. The material planning as well as accounting details are affected during transfers of goods between plants. In cases of plant-to-plant transfer, the accounting data of the two stocks is affected if they are assigned to different valuations. In other words, if there are any changes in the value of the stock items from the source plant to the destination plant, the accounting entries need to be adjusted accordingly. In this case, the stock value and G/L accounts need to be updated. Materials planning is also affected, because the stock transfer is scheduled and implemented according to the guidelines in materials planning. Plant-to-plant stock transfer is done by the one-step or two-step procedure but only the one-step procedure can be planned with a reservation.

49. How is stock transferred from company code to company code?

- Stock transfer between different company codes is done in a way similar to plant-to-plant transfer, but differs in the company code. During the stock transfer process, two accounting statements are created, one for removal of stock from the source company and the other for receiving the stock at the destination company.

50.   What is material-to-material transfer?

■ Over time, a material can change from the standard features defined in the master records and behave similarly to other materials. In these cases, a transfer posting from one material to another material is done. This type of posting is generally done in cases of pharmaceutical or chemical production units.

51.   How is stock transferred and posted using the stock determination functions?

■ When the material is withdrawn from one location for transfer to another location or from one stock to another stock according to a plan, you can determine the actual stock for the transfer of goods.

52.   How are the material documents for stock transfer created?

■ Material documents are created in the case of stock transfer by using one-step as well as two-step transfers. During one-step transfer, two material documents are created for every item that is transferred. The first is created for the removal of the goods at the issuing point and another is created for placing goods into storage at the receiving point. Also, the items are displayed in the material documents.

■ During a two-step transfer, two documents are created. The first is created for the removal of the goods at the issuing point and another is created for placing goods into storage at the receiving point. Upon placement of the goods at the receiving point a material document is created. For every item entered, only one material document is created since the quantity is transferred from in stock transfer into unrestricted stock at the receiving end.

53. State the difference between the one-step and two-step procedures in stock transfer.

■ The differences between the one-step and two-step procedures are listed in the following table:

One-Step Procedure	Two-Step Procedure
A procedure for stock transfers.	Also a procedure for stock transfers.
The transfer of goods follows from an issuing point to a receiving point.	The transfer of goods follows from an issuing point to a receiving point.
The advantage of the one-step procedure is that only a single transaction is entered.	In a two-step procedure, two transactions are entered, one at the issuing point and one at the receiving point.
The monitoring of stock transfer is not required.	The monitoring of stock transfer is required.
The stock does not appear as "in stock transfer."	After the goods issued are posted at the issuing point, the stock appears as "in stock transfer" at the receiving end and is managed by that system.
To carry out a transfer from plant to plant for a material that is split valued, one-step procedure is used.	A transfer from plant to plant for a material that is split valued can not be done with a two-step procedure.

54. What is meant by the term "reservation"?

■ Reservation is the process of preemptive allocation of goods for later activities. The purpose of the reservation is to streamline the flow of material supply in case there is an adverse situation. Reservations of the goods are made in accordance with an order, cost center demand, or other related parameters. The reservation process is done in accordance with MRP. Apart from scheduling a goods issue or receipt, reservations can be made for planning the goods issue or receipt. Information about the type, quantity, and source of material, the proposed date of delivery, and the customer of the material is used in a reservation. Only one movement type and one account assignment object is created per reservation. A reservation document consists of a header and items. The header contains general data about the reservation such as preparing authority, movement type, and assignment of account. A single reservation is created for each purpose.

■ Reservation of items is done at the production or storage-allocation level. Reservations can be done either manually or by an automatic process. Automatic reservations are of two types. The first category consists of reservations for orders, networks, or projects; the second category covers stock transfer reservations done when the available stock on hand falls below the reorder point and the system generates a stock transfer reservation for the plant for the replenishment of quantity. Only one reservation is created for each purpose. Also, only one movement type is entered and only one accounting assignment is done.

55.   What is the purpose of a reservation?

■ The purpose of a reservation is to make sure that a material is available when it is required. You can reserve a material for a cost center, plant, or order.

■ The reservation process is followed by some events in the system. The first is the creation of the reservation document. In the material master record, the reserved quantity increases the reserved stock; however the total stock and unrestricted stock of the material remain unchanged. In MRP, the available stock is reduced by the reserved quantity. An entry is made in the MRP file as a result of the reservation. You can use two functions to display reserved stock. The stock overview at the plant level shows the total reserved stock for that material at the plant level. From the stock overview, select Environment > Reservations to display a list of the reservations for the material. Alternatively, the current stock/requirement list used by the system lists all of the open reservations for the material at the plant level and the reserved quantity of that material.

56.   What is physical inventory?

- Physical inventory is the recording of the actual stock levels (quantities) of materials by counting, weighing, or measuring them at a given storage location at a specific time.

57.   What is stock posting?

- Stock posting is defined as a transaction that occurs when you update an item quantity in the system, for example, updating the database after a goods issue or goods receipt.

58.   How is the value of cross-company-code stock displayed?

- You need to use the following navigation path to display the value of cross-company-code stock in transit: *Environment > Stock > Stock in Transit.*

59.   Describe the process of physical inventory count.

- Physical inventory count is the process of ascertaining the quantity of stock-in-hand using methods such as counting, weighing, and measuring, and recording of the results in the system. Follow these steps to perform a physical inventory count:
  - ☐ Process and post all the transactions that cause any changes in the inventory count (for example, goods receipts, inventory adjustments, transfer postings, and sales orders). All these steps should be taken care of in proper order to keep the inventory transaction history properly sequenced.
  - ☐ Keep intact all the materials that are to be counted in the warehouse.
  - ☐ Set aside the materials that are part of sales orders, but are still present in the warehouse.
  - ☐ Cease all movement of the stock in the warehouse.
  - ☐ Cease all transactions in the warehouse.

- ☐ Implement a stock-on-hand report for the material items to be counted. You can use the transaction code MB52 to generate this report. As a result, a screen appears that shows all the details regarding materials in the storage location that are in unrestricted quantities, in quality inspection, and in block quantities.

60. How can we prepare the inventory count difference list in SAP?

- ■ You can prepare the inventory count difference list with the help of transaction code MI20. You can also prepare this list by following the path: *SAP Menu > Logistics > Materials Management > Physical Inventory > Difference > Difference List.* As a result, the *List of Inventory Differences* screen appears. When you enter the selection information in the screen, a report is run. As a result, the materials from the selection are shown. The report identifies the quantity of the material, the counted quantity, and the differences, if any exist. Finally, once the differences are identified the count is repeated again to be sure, then the differences are posted as approved by management.

61. How can we post a count document?

- ■ You can post a count document either by typing the transaction code MI07 or by accessing the following navigation path: *SAP Menu > Logistics > Materials Management > Physical Inventory > Difference > Post.*
- ■ Remember that the physical document number must be entered along with the posting date and threshold value.

62. How can we post a count in the SAP system without a physical count document?

- ■ You can post a count without a physical count document either by using the transaction code MI10 or by accessing the following navigation path: *SAP Menu > Logistics >*

Materials Management > Physical Inventory > Difference > Enter w/o Document Reference. The inventory user can directly enter the count in the transaction, which is immediately posted. The inventory user can add single line items that have been counted, in addition to the amount pertaining to each line item. If the amount entered is out of range, the user is warned with a message that the amount entered is greater than the allowed precision. Finally, once all the material line items are entered, the document is posted.

63. How are inventory differences accounted for?

■ When inventory differences are posted, the total stock is automatically adjusted in the document. When the document is posted, the differences in the inventory will be either in the category of a goods issue or a goods receipt. If the counted quantity is less than the inventory, the stock account is credited with the value of the inventory difference. The accounting entry is then posted to the expense from the physical inventory account.

■ In contrast, if the counted quantity exceeds the inventory balance, then the stock account is debited with the value of the inventory difference. The accounting entry is then posted to the income from the physical inventory account.

64. Define the process of creating the physical inventory.

■ The process of physical inventory creation can be divided into three phases.
  □ Physical inventory preparation:
    ▪ Creating a physical inventory document
    ▪ Blocking materials for posting
    ▪ Printing and distributing the physical inventory document
  □ Physical inventory count:
    ▪ Counting stocks
    ▪ Entering the result of the count on the physical inventory document printout

- □ Physical inventory analysis:
  - ▪ Entering the result of the count into the system
  - ▪ Initiating a recount if necessary
- ▪ The physical inventory creation process can be done in the following three steps:
  - □ Creating the physical inventory document
  - □ Counting the physical inventory
  - □ Posting the difference in the inventory
- ▪ The preceding steps of physical inventory creation can be also done in combination in a single step. First, the physical inventory count with reference to the physical inventory document is posted. The physical inventory count with the inventory difference according to the previous inventory document is then given. Then, the inventory count with reference to the physical inventory document is posted.
- ▪ After the creation of the physical inventory by any of the processes, the next step is to monitor the inventory status. This is done by recording each step of physical inventory creation in the particular inventory document. The inventory history and document header item of the inventory document are the major sources of information for monitoring inventory.
- ▪ When the differences in the inventory status of the item are input into the system, it is adjusted, and it corresponds to the actual value of the inventory.

65.   What are the special stocks in inventory management?

- ▪ Special stocks are defined as the stocks that must be managed separately by the company. They can be either company-owned or external stocks. There is a provision of special stocks related to external parties in inventory management, such as customers or vendors. They are managed separately from other stocks and divided into the following types:
  - □ Consignment
  - □ Subcontracting
  - □ Stock transfer using a stock transfer order
  - □ Third-party processing

> □ Returnable transport packaging
>
> □ Pipeline handling
>
> □ Sales order stock
>
> □ Project stock

■ In the SAP R/3 system, the following external stocks are available:

> □ *Stock of material issued to vendor*—Consists of the company's own stock provided to the vendor to manufacture the products.
>
> □ *Consignment stock at customer*—The stock of items at the customer's end.
>
> □ *Returnable packaging stock at customer*—The packaging materials supplied to the customer along with the products.

66. What are externally-owned special stocks?

■ Externally-owned stocks are related to a vendor or customer. In the SAP R/3 system, the different types of the externally-owned stocks are as follows:

> □ *Consignment*—Material belonging to the vendor that is stored on the company's premises.
>
> □ *Returnable transport packaging*—A medium wherein goods can be transported between vendors and customers.
>
> □ *Sales order*—Used with sales orders.
>
> □ *Project stock*—Stock held to complete a project.

■ Externally-owned stocks are allocated to the following different stock types:

> □ Unrestricted use
>
> □ Quality inspection
>
> □ Blocked stock

67. Define "procurement types."

■ The classifications that indicate the type of material procurement are called the procurement types. They indicate whether a material is procured using internal procurement, external procurement, or both.

■ The procurement process generally combines buying a material from a vendor and delivering the same to the company or concerned buyer. In some cases, the procurement of material is not generally routed from a buyer to a customer, but is directed toward a third party for intermediate processing, from where it is delivered to the customer. In the case of stock transfer processing, the goods are procured and transferred internally from the source to the destination location. The procurement types allowed in SAP are as follows:

- ☐ *Consignment*—The goods that are procured from a vendor on consignment. The goods are stored at the customer and belong to the vendors until they are consumed.

- ☐ *Subcontracting*—The vendor receives the goods from the producer and manufactures them at their end. The number of components to be manufactured is specified in the purchase order and provided to the subcontractor.

- ☐ *Stock transfer using a stock transfer order*—The goods are supplied within the company, from one plant to another. A special purchase order called a stock transfer order is generated for the stock transfer procurement type. The delivery of the good is processed in inventory management or sales and distribution.

- ☐ *Third-party processing*—This type of materials procurement is not generally routed from a buyer to a customer, but is directed toward a third party for intermediate processing, from where it is delivered to the customer.

- ☐ *Pipeline handling*—This is a type of procurement in which there are no requirements for ordering and storage of the material. For example, in the case of electricity generation, the continuous production and consumption of the material is done on a regular basis.

68. Name the documents posted during goods movements in inventory management and list the codes.

■ In Inventory Management, the following goods movements are posted:

- ☐ Initial entry of stock balances—561, 563
- ☐ Transfer posting from plant to plant in one step—301
- ☐ Transfer posting from material to material—309

69. How is vendor consignment useful?

- The material purchased from a vendor but not transferred to the customer's valuated stock is called vendor consignment. This stock is stored at the customer's location but remains the vendor's property until the customer transfers the stock to its valuated stock. Consignment stocks from the vendors are available for MRP.

70. What is returnable transport packaging (RTP)?

- RTP is a medium used to transport goods between vendors and customers. Once the goods are received, the returnable packaging is returned to the vendor. The best example is the crate for cold drinks; it needs to be returned after receipt of the drinks.

71. What is sales order stock?

- The stock assigned to a sales order but still available in the company premises is called the sales order stock.
- Raw materials ordered by the customer for processing a specific order and finished goods come under the category of sales order stock.

72. What is project stock?

- The stock available in the company premises to execute a project is called the project stock. It is assigned to a work breakdown structure element and is specific to the project only. All accounting treatment in MM is done for the specific project head.

CHAPTER 7
LOGISTICS
INVOICE
VERIFICATION

LOGISTICS INVOICE VERIFICATION

1.   What does the term LIV mean?

■ LIV stands for Logistics Invoice Verification. It is the last component of the logistics supply chain that is comprised of purchasing, inventory management, and invoice verification in materials management (MM). In invoice verification, the comparison of vendor invoices is performed with respect to purchase orders and goods receipts. The vendor invoices are also checked on the basis of the following three parameters:

   □ Content

   □ Price

   □ Quantity

■ When the posting of the invoice is performed, the data of the invoices is stored and saved in the system and, finally, the data saved in the invoice documents is updated, and is reflected in MM and financial accounting.

2. What are the main features of LIV?

- Being a part of MM, LIV offers the following features:
  - □ It involves the whole process of materials procurement, which starts with raw material purchase and ends with the finished goods receipt.
  - □ It permits the creation of invoices, for example, services, course costs, and expenses, that are not created in the materials procurement process.
  - □ It involves processing the credit memos in the form of either invoice reversals or return deliveries.

3. What is invoice verification?

- Invoice verification is used to store details of vendor invoices and is an important part of purchasing and inventory management. It consists of entering invoices and credit memos, checking the accuracy of invoices in accordance with price, and checking block invoices.

4. What are the different types of invoice verification?

- The different types of invoice verification are as follows:
  - □ Invoices based on purchase orders
  - □ Invoices based on goods receipts
  - □ Invoices without an order reference

5. What is the transaction code for invoice verification?

- An invoice is verified using the OLMR transaction code.

6. How can we perform invoice verification?

- Invoice verification is the process of checking the accuracy of an invoice in terms of the quantity, price, and other related information. An invoice can be issued for several processes. For example, if an invoice is issued for a purchase order, then the system checks for the relevant information, such as vendor, material, quantity, delivery date, and payment details.

7. How can we process an invoice verification?

- Processing an invoice verification involves the following:
  - ☐ Online invoice verification
  - ☐ Parking
  - ☐ Invoice verification in the background
  - ☐ Automatic settlement
  - ☐ Invoices received through EDI
- These are explained below.

Online Invoice Verification

- In the case of online invoice verification, a user receives the invoice, analyzes it, and feeds the information contained in the invoice into the system. A comparison of the data contained within the invoice is performed per the system specifications and suggestions, and if there are any discrepancies in the comparative study, the necessary corrections are made in the invoices. After this, the invoice is posted.

Parking

- In the case of parking, a user receives the invoice, analyzes it, and then feeds the information contained within the invoice into the system and saves it. Necessary changes are then made in the invoice document as desired by the user, and after saving the changes, the invoice is posted.

Invoice Verification in the Background

- In the case of invoice verification in the background, a user receives the invoice and then feeds the complete data of the invoice into the system. The invoice is then compared with the invoice in the other system. The system then carries out the necessary checks in the invoice, but this checking is performed in the background. If no errors arise during the checking process, the checked and error-free invoice is posted in the background. If any errors in the invoice arise, the system saves the invoice, and then the processing of the invoice is performed later.

Automatic Settlement

■ Automatic settlement is further classified into the following four types:

  □ Evaluated receipt settlement

  □ Consignment and pipeline settlement

  □ Invoicing plan

  □ Revaluation

■ These are explained below.

  □ Evaluated receipt settlement:

    ▪ In this case, a user prepares an invoice and posts it on the basis of the purchase orders and receipts of the goods. Vendors do not provide any invoices to the user.

  □ Consignment and pipeline settlement:

    ▪ In this case, similar to evaluated receipt settlement, the vendor does not contribute in providing the invoice. All posted withdrawals are handled by the user himself and, after successful settlement, a settlement statement is sent to the vendor for further inquiry.

  □ Invoicing plan:

    ▪ In the case of an invoicing plan, a user does not need to to wait every time for the invoices for supplied goods and performed services sent by the vendor. In such situations, the user creates invoices based on the dates scheduled in the purchase order form. Ultimately, payment is made to the vendor on the basis of these invoices.

  □ Revaluation:

    ▪ Revaluation analyzes different values based on changes in the prices of the goods. On the basis of these values, settlement documents are created and finally posted to the vendor.

Invoices Received Through EDI

■ In this case, all the information contained within the invoice is exchanged with the system electronically by using electronic data interchange (EDI) and, finally, the invoice is posted and checked automatically. If any errors arise, manual error-checking is done in the invoice to remove the errors.

8. What are the main steps in the invoice verification process?

■ Invoice verification is a part of the accounts payment process in which the company pays the vendor for the materials and services provided to the company. The invoice verification process ensures that the quantity and pricing are entered correctly. Invoice verification uses a standard method called three-way match, which requires the purchase order, goods receipt, and invoice. You can perform the following steps to enter an invoice into the system:

  ☐ Select *SAP Menu > Logistics > Materials Management > Logistics Invoice Verification > Document Entry > Enter Invoice.* This opens the Enter Company Code dialog box.

  ☐ Enter the company code in the company code text box and click the Enter button. This opens the *Enter Incoming Invoice: Company Code XXXX* page, where XXXX is the code of the company.

  ☐ Enter the invoice date in the invoice date text box. The date should not extend beyond the current date. The posting date is set to the current date but you can change it as required.

  ☐ Enter the amount in the amount text box as displayed on the invoice provided by the vendor.

  ☐ Select the calculate tax check box to calculate the tax automatically when the invoice is posted.

  ☐ Enter the purchase order number. This displays the details in the purchase order reference tab.

  ☐ Click the Enter button on the toolbar. An information box appears.

  ☐ Click the Continue (Enter) button to complete the process.

  ☐ Click the Exit button on the toolbar until you return back to the SAP Easy Access page.

9. Define ERS.

■ ERS stands for evaluated receipts settlement. It refers to the process of settling down receipts of the goods in an automatic manner. In this process, the vendor and the user agree that vendors do not prepare any invoices for the goods ordered. Rather, the system will automatically generate and post the invoice document on the basis of the purchase order and receipts of goods. ERS also offers the following advantages:

- □ Using ERS, all purchasing transactions are quickly closed.

- □ Errors of communication are avoided.

- □ Invoice verification is not prone to price and quantity variances.

10. Invoice verification is done with reference to which documents?

■ In SAP, invoice verification is done on the basis of the following:

- □ Document date, purchase order number, invoice amount, tax amount, and terms of payment (if required)

- □ Purchase order, which includes vendors, terms of payment (if required), currency, and invoice items

- □ Purchase order history, which includes quantity and amount

- □ SAP R/3 system settings, which include the rate at which the tax is calculated

- □ Vendor master record, which includes bank information

11. What is a parked invoice document?

■ A parked invoice document is one in which you can enter the invoice data or the credit memo data in the computer system and then save it. However, the system cannot post it initially. The final invoice is posted only after all of the changes are incorporated in the document. Data is saved in the system with the help of a function called park incoming invoice. Parking of the invoice is done only for the following reasons:

□ All the invoice information required for posting is not complete, that is, some information is missing. For instance, the balance is not zero.

□ The process of invoice data entry is performed at different levels involving several persons, such as clerks and invoice verification department personnel.

■ Always keep in mind that when you park the documents, you must ensure that all the following parameters are properly entered and checked:

□ Date of the document

□ Invoicing party

□ Vendor

□ Account assignment objects

■ During parking, the following updates take place in the invoice:

□ Document changes

□ Data for advance tax returns

□ Index for duplicate invoice check

□ Vendor open items

□ Purchase order history

■ All of these updates are incorporated into the parked invoice document. After that, the updated parked invoice document is no longer on hold and is ready for posting.

12.   How do we park an invoice?

■ You can park an invoice using the MIR7 transaction code. Perform the following steps to park an invoice:

□ Select *SAP Menu > Logistics > Materials Management > Logistics Invoice Verification > Document Entry > Park Invoice.* The *Enter Company Code* dialog box opens.

□ Enter the company code in the company code text box.

□ Press the Enter button. This opens the *Park Incoming Invoice: Company Code XXXX* page where XXXX is the company code.

□ Select invoice from the transaction drop-down list, if not selected.

□ Enter the appropriate details in the fields under different tabs.

□ Click the Save button on the toolbar.

13. What is the benefit of document parking?

■ The benefit of document parking is that you can modify an invoice in a parked status, whereas an invoice that is placed on hold cannot be modified.

14. How do we display the parked document?

■ You can display the parked documents by using either FB03 or FBV3. The FB03 transaction code displays all the posted documents, whereas the FBV3 code shows only the parked documents that have not been posted to the expenditure balance.

15. What is posting an invoice? How is it different from parking an invoice?

■ Posting an invoice refers to the process of placing the transactions of the invoice into the purchase account, whereas parking an invoice means the user receives the invoice, analyzes it, and then feeds the information contained within the invoice into the system and saves it. Necessary changes are then made in the invoice document as desired by the user, and, after saving the changes, the invoice is posted.

16. What is a credit memo?

■ A credit memo represents the receipt that contains information regarding the sale of the product or services issued by the supplier to the purchaser. It also contains the authenticity of the prices of the variety of products and commodities sold by the supplier. It is context-based and varies per the different modules of the SAP system. Credit memos involve a posting that brings down the balance of receivables or payables. Also, for sales and distribution (SD) and supplier relationship management (SRM), they involve a document that lessens the bill related to a party's obligations, the vendor, and the service agent. The credit memo is most likely created only in the cases where the supplier delivered defective goods, provided bad service, or, last but not least, overcharged for the goods.

■ A credit memo is comprised of the preliminary credit memo information, such as total tax, freight costs, total amount, vendor, and invoice recipient information, and also detailed credit memo information that constitutes header information, item information, and approval preview.

17. What are subsequent debit and subsequent credit?

■ In the case of subsequent debit, the vendor provides the invoice to the user for all of the goods received. Transportation costs are also taken into account, but the quantity of invoices remains the same.

■ In the case of subsequent credit, the vendor provides the credit memo to the user for all of the goods received.

18. Define "invoice status."

■ Invoice status is the extent to which the invoice has been processed. The different statuses for an invoice are as follows:

Status	Meaning
Scheduled for background verification	Schedules the invoice to be verified in the background. This type of invoice status can be saved online using the application Enter Invoice for Invoice Verification in the Background, or by using an earlier release of an older invoice that was converted.

Status	Meaning
Verified as incorrect	Verifies the invoice in the background, but does not post the invoice because the difference in the data entries in the invoice is very large. Alternately, there arises an error when verification is done in the background, for instance if the settings of the system are not up to par. As a result the invoice is kept online using the Enter Invoice for Invoice Verification in the Background.
Correct (posted, not completed)	Posts the invoice successfully with the help of invoice verification in the background. The demarcation between the invoices is also posted online and is made in the background.
Posted	Posts the invoice online. Correct verification of the invoice is done in the background and later the status of the invoices is changed.

19. What is stochastic blocking?

■ Stochastic blocking is the process of checking incoming invoices. In this process, blocking the invoices is done randomly. Invoices with high value have the highest probability to be blocked. The invoice is instead set at the item level. When the invoice is posted, an "R" is set in the payment block field in the document header data.

20. How can we manually block an invoice?

■ You can manually an invoice in either of the following two ways:
   □ By entering an "R" in the Payment Field block in the document header data.

□ By making use of the "ma" (manual blocking reason) field in the item list.

Note: Take into account that manually blocked items give the reason for blocking as manual block (M).

21.   What is total-based invoice reduction?

■ Total-based invoice reduction is a function that is helpful in cases of vendors who often send overpriced invoices. Whenever you use total-based invoice reduction, you should take into consideration the following points:

□ It specifies the list of vendors for which total-based invoice reduction is used.

□ It is helpful if you are convinced that differences in the invoice occur due to vendor errors.

□ It determines the cases where manual invoice reduction is more helpful.

□ It is helpful in situations when the cost for error searching exceeds the gain.

22.   What are the different accounts used in invoicing?

■ The different accounts used in invoicing are as follows:

□ Vendor accounts
□ Stock accounts
□ GR/IR clearing accounts
□ Tax accounts
□ Price differences accounts
□ Cash difference-clearing accounts
□ Freight-clearing accounts

23.   How do we enter the planned delivery cost in an invoice?

■ The vendor, carrier, and custom office decide upon planned delivery costs before the creation of the purchase order.

After this, they are entered into the purchase order. Entering delivery costs in an invoice involves the following steps:

☐ Enter the data of the header per the requirements of the LIV screen.

☐ Compare the invoice with the following:

  ▪ Purchase order/scheduling

  ▪ Delivery note

  ▪ Bill of lading

  ▪ Vendor

☐ On the basis of your allocation, enter the document number or the vendor.

☐ From the list field, specify the items that you want to display:

  ▪ Planned delivery costs

  ▪ Goods items, service items, and planned delivery goods

☐ Select the tick sign. The system then proposes the invoice items.

☐ Check that the invoice items selected match those of the invoice. If there is a discrepancy, change the selection accordingly.

☐ Compare the quantities and amounts in the delivery costs items with those of invoice. If any variances occur, you can either accept them or the system may sometimes reduce the invoice.

☐ Select Save Post.

24.   How are quantity and price variances entered?

■ Quantity or price variances are entered in the following ways:

  ☐ Accepting the difference

  ☐ Reducing the invoice

■ These are explained below.

Accepting the Difference

■ If you want to accept the difference, certain changes must be made in the quantity and value as suggested by the system.

When the invoice is posted, the system bases the account movements on the changed data.

Reducing the Invoice

■ If you do not want to accept the difference, you enter the quantity in separate fields and the difference is marked as a vendor error. When the invoice is posted, two documents are created by the system. One document posts the invoice items by using the default data and vendor line with the help of the actual invoice amount. The other document enters the credit memo, which acts as a complaint document for the difference. As a result, during a payment run only the actual amount is fetched as expected by the system. In addition, using the unchanged default data, the purchase order history is updated.

---

25.   How do we post an invoice?

■ In LIV, you can post invoices that have or do not have purchase order references. The SAP system provides the following two options to post an invoice:

  ☐ Posting an invoice to a general ledger (G/L) account

  ☐ Posting an invoice to a material account

■ *Posting an invoice to a G/L account*—You can post an invoice to a G/L account with or without a purchase order reference.

■ To post an invoice to a G/L account without a purchase order reference, perform the following steps:

  ☐ Select *SAP Menu > Logistics > Materials Management > Logistics Invoice Verification > Document Entry > Enter Invoice or Park Invoice.*

  ☐ Enter the header data that is required.

  ☐ In the header data, click the details tab and in the invoice party field, enter the invoicing party number.

  ☐ Select the G/L account tab and enter the required data, such as the G/L account number, credit or debit posting, amounts, and account assignment information.

  ☐ Select Post.

- To post an invoice to a G/L account that has a purchase order reference, perform the following steps:
  - □ Select *SAP Menu > Logistics > Materials Management > Logistics Invoice Verification > Document Entry > Enter Invoice or Park Invoice.*
  - □ Enter the header data that is required.
  - □ Now assign the invoice to a document and check the items that need to be settled.
  - □ Select the G/L account tab and enter the required data, such as G/L account number, credit or debit posting, amounts, account assignment information.
  - □ Select Post.
- *Posting an invoice to a material account*—You can post an invoice to a material account with or without a purchase order reference. To post an invoice to a material account without a purchase order reference, perform the following steps:
  - □ Select *SAP Menu > Logistics > Materials Management > Logistics Invoice Verification > Document Entry > Enter Invoice or Park Invoice.*
  - □ Enter the header data that is required.
  - □ In the header data, click the details tab and in the inv. party field enter the invoicing party number.
  - □ Select the material tab and enter the required data, such as material number and plant.
  - □ Select Post.
- To post an invoice to a material account having a purchase order reference, perform the following steps:
  - □ Select *SAP Menu > Logistics > Materials Management > Logistics Invoice Verification > Document Entry > Enter Invoice or Park Invoice.*
  - □ Enter the header data that is required.
  - □ Assign the invoice to a document and check the items that need to be settled.
  - □ Select the material tab and enter the required data such as material number, plant, valuation type (if required), credit or debit posting, and amount.
  - □ Select Post.

26. What are the different types of variances in invoices? Describe them.

- The different types of variances in invoices are listed and described as follows:
  - □ *Quantity variance*—There is a difference between the quantity mentioned in the invoice and the quantity delivered.
  - □ *Price variance*—There is a difference between the price mentioned in the invoice and in the purchase order.
  - □ *Quantity and price variance*—There are differences in both the quantity and price.
  - □ *Order price quantity variance*—There is a difference between the price per ordered quantity, for example, if $50 per piece is mentioned on the purchase order but the invoice says $60 per piece.

27. Why do invoices get blocked?

- Invoices can be blocked for the following reasons:
  - □ Variance in the invoice item
  - □ Amount of an invoice item
  - □ Stochastic block
  - □ Manual block

28. What happens when an invoice is blocked? What are the different ways to block an invoice?

- When an invoice is blocked, the invoice amount cannot be paid to the vendor. Blocking an invoice also blocks the individual items. The different ways to block an invoice are listed as follows:
  - □ Manual block
  - □ Stochastic or random block
  - □ Block due to amount of an invoice item
  - □ Block due to variance of an invoice item

29. How do we release an invoice?

■ When an invoice is blocked, you can release it by cancelling the blocking indicator that was set when the invoice was originally posted. An invoice can also be released automatically using the MRBR transaction code. The automatic process deletes all the selected items that no longer apply to the invoice. You can start the transaction to release an invoice using the path: *SAP Menu > Logistics > Materials Management > Logistics Invoice Verification > Further Processing > Release Blocked Invoices.*

30. How can we post an invoice directly without any references?

■ When posting invoices without a reference, proposed values for the invoiced items are not displayed by the system, because the system does not determine any purchase order items or a posted goods receipt for the invoice. As a consequence, information related to the accounts changed by the offsetting entry for the vendor line item is not found in the database of the system.

31. How does the SAP system validate the data of an incoming invoice?

■ Data of an incoming invoice is validated by the SAP system by using the following data:
  □ Master data
  □ Transaction data

Master Data

■ Refers to the data that is permanent for the materials in the SAP system. Each and every object is provided a unique number by which the object is identified in the system.
■ Master data is of the following types:
  □ Material data
  □ Vendor data
  □ Accounting data
■ These types of data are described below.

Material data

■ Information based on materials bought by the company or produced in the company. This data is comprised of material number, material name, units of measure, stock data, and over- and under-delivery tolerances. Various departments within MM maintain material data.

Vendor data

■ Information related to suppliers with whom the company deals. Vendor data is comprised of data such as address, bank data, and probably also the name of the head office or bank. Vendor data is maintained by the purchasing and accounting departments.

Accounting data

■ Used to define the G/L account. It is comprised of data such as the account name, the account type, and the currency in which the account is managed. Financial accounting maintains the accounting data.

Transaction Data

■ Records the transactions in SAP systems. On the basis of the purchase order, scheduling agreement, goods receipt, or invoice, the system creates a document automatically. Each document is identified on the basis of the document number. These documents are of the following types:

  ☐ Purchasing document

  ☐ Material document

  ☐ Accounting document

■ These are discussed in detail below.

Purchasing documents

■ Contains information pertaining to the vendor number, purchase order date, terms of delivery, material number, and order quantity.

Material documents

■ These documents are created only when the receipt of the goods is posted. It is comprised of data such as posting date and quantity delivered.

Accounting documents

■ These documents are created when a goods receipt or invoice is posted (unless the goods receipt is not valuated). Details of individual postings along with account number, posting key, and the amount are contained in this document.

32. What do the W, V, and F fields show in the status of a document in FBV3?

- The W field indicates that the document is a workflow document and is related to cash deposits. The V field indicates that the document is complete and has been sent to workflow for approval. The F field indicates that it has been approved and posted for expenditure.

33. What is the menu path to create a document or e-mail notification for your supplier?

- The menu path to create a document/e-mail notification for your supplier is as follows: *Material Management > Logistics Invoice Verification > Message Determination*.

34. What are invoice tolerances? How can we post small differences?

- Invoice tolerances are often the differences between the invoice amount and payment amount, or sometimes it refers to the differences between the goods receipt amount and invoice amount. However, always keep in mind that this difference is acceptable to the client. An invoice is posted only if the balance is zero.
- If a minimal difference in the values of total debit and credit arises, it will lead to higher time, cost, and effort to analyze the reason behind the difference. After analyzing the reason, individual items are then changed.

35. What is the difference between GR-based IV and PO-based IV?

- GR-based IV means goods receipt-based invoice verification. In this process, each receipt of the individual goods is invoiced separately.

■ On the other hand, PO-based IV means purchase order-based invoice verification. In this process, all the items in the purchase order list are arranged and placed together. It does not take into consideration whether the item is received in a single delivery or multiple deliveries. After all the items are collected, they are posted in the form of one single item.

36. What are the planned delivery costs involved in purchasing?

■ Delivery costs refer to the costs that are invoiced for the delivery over and above the value of the delivery itself. This is comprised of freight charges, customs duty, or other costs. Planned delivery cost is one of the types of delivery costs. These are entered on the basis of items in the purchase order. Certain provisions are made for relevent costs of the goods receipts. When the invoice is entered, the planned delivery costs specified in the purchase order are referenced. Purchase order history acts as a reference for the values of the items proposed.

37. How are taxes posted at the time of invoice verification?

■ Taxes are posted at the time of invoice verification by performing the following steps:

  □ Select *Logistics Invoice Verification > Document Entry > Enter Invoice*. As a result, the *Enter Invoice* screen appears.

  □ Enter the header data as per the requirement, then enter the tax amount, and then select the tax code from the list field.

■ If required, you can change any tax codes proposed by the system.

  □ If the amount of tax is not entered in the invoice, leave the tax amount field blank and select the calculate tax field.

  □ Match the invoice with any other system document.

  □ Select Continue.

■ The system then suggests the invoice items. The system automatically suggests a tax code either from the order item or G/L account.

☐ In case the entries are incorrect and we select Simulate or Post, the Tax Data screen appears. A Tax Data screen includes the following:

- All tax codes in the session
- All previously entered tax amounts
- The tax base for each tax code

■ You can make corrections to the tax amounts. If you do not enter the tax amounts and tax codes on the LIV screen, the missing tax codes contained in the items are displayed. You have to enter the relevant amount on the basis of these tax codes. The system does not make your entries here. The system only checks the tax amount, the tax code, and the base amount after the selection of the post or simulate functions.

■ In addition, you cannot change the tax base on the Tax Data screen. If this is wrong, the amount or the tax code is also entered incorrectly in the item. Finally, you have to go to the invoice items to make the necessary corrections.

☐ Select Continue.

■ As a result, the LIV screen reappears.

CHAPTER 8
VALUATION
AND ACCOUNT
ASSIGNMENT

VALUATION AND ACCOUNT ASSIGNMENT

1.   How can we create the vendor account group in SAP?

- You can perform the following steps to create the vendor account group in *SAP: Select Display IMG > Financial Accounting > Accounts Payable/Receivable > Vendor Accounts > Master Records > Preparation of Creating Vendor Master Records > Define Accounts Groups with Screen Layout/Define Screen Layout Per Activity.*

2.   What is the purpose of material valuation?

- Material valuation in the SAP materials management (MM) module is necessary to determine the stock value of materials.

3.   How do we determine the stock value?

- The stock value of materials is calculated using the following formula:

  Stock value = Stock quantity * Material price

4. How is material valuation associated with financial accounting?

■ Material valuation in the MM module is associated with financial accounting because any change in the stock value also updates the general ledger (G/L) account in the Financial Accounting module.

5. What factors control material valuation?

■ The factors that control material valuation are:
  □ System settings
  □ Material master record

6. What is the valuation area?

■ The valuation area is the organizational level at which material valuation is carried out.

7. What is the difference between the valuation area at the company code level and at the plant level?

■ You can define the valuation area at either the company code level or at the plant level. If you define the valuation area at the company code level, all the stock of a particular company is valuated together. If you define the valuation area at the plant level, all the stock of a particular material in the individual plant is valuated together. In this case, the stocks of the other plants are not included.

8. Define "valuation class."

■ A valuation class is a group of different materials that share some common properties. This group is defined so that you do not have to manage a separate account for each material.

9. How is a valuation class configured?

- A valuation class is a way of assigning a material to G/L accounts. You can configure a valuation class by performing the following steps:
  - □ Open the SAP Implementation guide.
  - □ Select *Materials Management > Valuation and Account Assignment > Account Determination > Account Determination Without Wizard > Define Valuation Classes*. This opens the *Account Category Reference/Valuation Classes* page.
  - □ Click the Valuation Class button. This opens the change view *Valuation Classes: Overview* page displaying the list of all the valuation classes.
  - □ Click the New Entries button. This opens the *New Entries: Overview of Added Entries* page.
  - □ Enter the appropriate data in the fields and click the Save button on the toolbar. This adds the new entry to the list.
  - □ Click the Exit button on the toolbar until you return back to the *Display IMG* page.

10. Explain material valuation with the moving average price.

- You can use the moving average price, which you get by dividing the value of the material by the total stock, to evaluate material. The moving average price changes when there is a goods movement that is relevant for material valuation. The accounting department sets the initial price entry to "V" when valuating material using the moving average price.
- The formula for calculating the new quantity, value, and price of the material when using moving average price is:

$$\text{Quantity}_{new} = \text{Quantity}_{old} + \text{Quantity}_{receipt}$$

$$\text{Value}_{new} = \text{Value}_{old} + \text{Quantity}_{receipt} \times (\text{Price}_{receipt}/\text{Price unit}_{receipt})$$

$$\text{Price}_{new} = (\text{Value}_{new}/\text{Quantity}_{new}) \times \text{Price unit}_{material\ master}$$

11. Explain material valuation with the standard price.

■ In comparison to the average price, which changes frequently, the standard price remains constant and does not change once entered. This means that it is not affected by any changes in the invoice price. The accounting department sets the initial price entry to "S" when valuating the material using the standard price.

■ The formula for calculating the new quantity, value, and price of the material when using standard price is:

$$\text{Quantity}_{new} = \text{Quantity}_{old} + \text{Quantity}_{receipt}$$
$$\text{Value}_{new} = \text{Value}_{old} + \text{Quantity}_{receipt} \times (\text{Price}_{material\ master} / \text{Price unit}_{material\ master})$$
$$\text{Price}_{new} = \text{Price}_{old} = \text{Price}_{material\ master}$$

12. What is the valuation level in the SAP system?

■ The valuation level in the SAP system is the level at which material stocks are evaluated as a whole for the client. You can define valuation level by using either the OX14 transaction code or by using the following navigation path: *IMG > Enterprise Structure > Definition > Logistics-General > Define Valuation Level*. You can evaluate the stock either at the plant level or the company code level.

13. What is the significance of an account assignment category?

■ An account assignment category determines the account assignment details that are required for the purchase order item, such as cost center or account number. It is useful in SAP MM as it helps determine the following:

☐ The type of account assignment

☐ The accounts that will be charged when you post the invoice or goods receipt

☐ The account assignment data that you should provide

14.   What are the account assignment categories?

- The account assignment categories are:
  - □ *Single account assignment*—Specifies one account assignment for an item in the purchase order.
  - □ *Multiple account assignment*—Allocates the costs associated with the purchase order item.

15.   How can we create a purchase requisition with single and multiple account assignments?

- In a single account assignment, you can specify only one account assignment for an item in the purchase order. After the item has been entered into the purchase order creation transaction, you can access the account assignment dialog box by selecting *Item > Account Assignment*. Now, you can enter the account assignment data, which is dependent on the account assignment category.
- In a multiple account assignment, you can allocate more than one account to one purchase order line. You can assign multiple accounts by performing the following steps:
  - □ Select *Item > Account Assignment*.
  - □ Enter the account assignment data for the first account assignment item.
  - □ Select Change Display. This displays the multiple account assignment screen.
  - □ Enter the relevant data in the items filed.
  - □ Repeat the previous step for the rest of the items.
  - □ Save the purchase order.

16.   How can we create a purchase order with reference to a purchase requisition with an account assignment?

- You can create a purchase order with reference to a purchase requisition with an account assignment using either the

ME21N transaction code or the following navigation path: *SAP Menu > Logistics > Materials Management > Purchasing > Purchase Order > Create > Vendor/Supplying Plant Known > Create Purchase Order*.

17. How can we maintain account assignment categories in the SAP system?

■ You can maintain account assignment categories in the SAP system by using the following navigation path: *IMG > Materials Management > Purchasing > Account Assignment > Maintain Account Assignment Categories*.

18. What is the balance sheet valuation?

■ The balance sheet valuation is the process of calculating the price of the materials in stock, which is then used in the balance sheet creation. The balance sheet valuation is done on the basis of country specific tax and commercial laws and the organization's accounting policies. The SAP system provides the following balance sheet valuation techniques:

  □ Lowest value determination

  □ LIFO (last in, first out) valuation

  □ FIFO (first in, first out) valuation

19. What is a LIFO valuation?

■ LIFO is a balance sheet valuation technique. It stands for the last in, first out principle, i.e., the material added to the stock last is valuated first. In this technique, the pricing of old material in stock is not affected by the pricing of new material. The valuation is done on the basis of a layer of stock, increased or decreased, created for a fiscal year. For example, if the stock is increased, then a new layer is created for that stock. However, to use LIFO, you have to configure it.

20. How can we configure a LIFO valuation?

■ You can configure a LIFO valuation by following these steps:

  □ *Activate the LIFO*—You can activate the LIFO valuation either by using the OMWE transaction code or by using the following menu path: *SAP Customizing Implementation Guide > Materials Management > Valuation and Account Assignment > Balance Sheet Valuation Procedures > Configure LIFO/FIFO Methods > General Information > Activate/Deactivate LIFO/FIFO Valuation.*

  □ *Configure the valuation area or company code*—You can configure the valuation area or the company code after activating the LIFO valuation by using the MRLH transaction code.

  □ *Configure the movement type*—After configuring the valuation area, you need to configure the material movement type. You can configure the material movement type by using the following menu path: *SAP Customizing Implementation Guide > Materials Management > Valuation and Account Assignment > Balance Sheet Valuation Procedures > Configure LIFO/FIFO Methods > General Information > Define LIFO/FIFO Relevant Movement Types.*

  □ *Configure the material master record*—The material you want to valuate must be marked for LIFO. You can mark the material for LIFO by using the following menu path: *SAP Menu > Logistics > Materials Management > Valuation > Balance Sheet Valuation > LIFO Valuation > Prepare > MRL6-Select Materials.*

  □ *Create base layers*—You can create base layers by using the following menu path: *SAP Menu > Logistics > Materials Management > Valuation > Balance Sheet Valuation > LIFO Valuation > Prepare > MRL8-Create Base Layer.*

  □ *Run the LIFO*—The last step is to run the LIFO. You can run the LIFO by using the following menu path: *SAP Menu > Logistics > Materials Management > Valuation > Balance Sheet Valuation > LIFO Valuation > Perform Check.*

21. What is a FIFO valuation?

- FIFO is a balance sheet valuation technique. It stands for first in, first out. In this technique, the material purchased or produced first is sold, consumed, or handled first. When the oldest materials are consumed, the new and more expensive materials remain as assets on the balance sheet. You can use this technique to evaluate the stocks of a material as realistically as possible. In this technique, the pricing of the material is done on the basis of the last stock received.

22. Briefly describe the types by which a material value is determined.

- The material value is determined by using the following value determination types:
  - □ *Market prices*—The material value is detemined based on the market prices. The system looks for the lowest price or the most recent price among the different prices stored for each material.
  - □ *Range of coverage*—The material value is determined based on the range of coverage. The system looks for whether a material's price should be devaluated because of its high range of coverage.
  - □ *Movement rate*—The material value is determined based on the movement rate. Here, the system determines if the price of a material should be devaluated because of slow movement or non-movement.
  - □ *Loss-free valuation*—The material value is detemined based on loss-free valuation. The system can devaluate a material if the material's price is not fetched while it is sold.

23. What is the importance of the material ledger?

- A ledger that keeps the information about material cost and pricing is called the material ledger. A material ledger has the following benefits:

    ☐ It helps valuate material in various currencies. However, to evaluate the material in various currencies, you have to activate the ledger.

    ☐ It helps determine the material's actual price.

24. What are the ways in which the material price can be determined?

■ The material price can be determined in the following ways:

    ☐ Single-level material price determination

    ☐ Multi-level material price determination

    ☐ Transaction-based material price determination

CHAPTER 9
RELEASE
PROCEDURES

RELEASE PROCEDURES

1. What is the release procedure?

- The release procedure allows you to create condition records for the planning process. It is used to create purchase requisitions (PRs), purchase orders (POs), requests for quotation (RFQs), outline agreements, and service entry sheets.

2. What is the release strategy? How many release points can be involved in a release process?

- The release strategy specifies the release codes with which a purchase document must be released and the sequence in which the release must be used. You can define a maximum of eight release codes with respective release strategies. You can involve eight release points in a release process.

3. Can you release the PO item by item when you have a multi-line-item PO?

- No, you cannot release the PO item by item. The PO can be released at the header level by using the classification release procedure.

4. How are the release procedures for PRs and POs defined?

■ The transaction codes ME54 and ME29N are used to define the release procedures for PRs and POs, respectively.

5. How are the release procedures configured?

■ The release procedures can be configured using the transaction code OMGQ in older versions. The navigation path is steps are as follows: *Materials Management > Purchasing > Purchase Requisition > Release Procedure > Procedure with Classification > Set Up Procedure.*

6. How do we release blocked purchase documents?

■ You can release a blocked purchase document by using your release code. This is called the release transaction. After you have released the document, you can cancel the document using the same release code.

7. How do we reject approvals in the SAP R/3 system? Will it affect the SAP business workflow?

■ You can use the ME54N transaction code for PRs and the ME29N transaction code for POs to reject approvals in the SAP R/3 software. This does not affect the SAP business workflow.

8. How many procedures are available to release PRs?

■ There are two types of procedures available to release PRs:
  □ *With classification*—In this procedure, you can release the PR both at item level and in total.
  □ *Without classification*—In this procedure, you can release the PR only at item level.

9. **How do we release POs? Which transaction code is used to display as well as reset the release of POs?**

■ You can release a PO at the header level. You cannot release a single item in a PO. You need to release all the items at the same time. You can use the ME29N transaction code to display as well as reset the release of POs.

10. **How many types of release procedures are available for POs?**

■ There are two types of release procedures available for POs:
  □ *Individual release*—In this type of release procedure, you can release only one item at a time.
  □ *Collective release*—In this type of release procedure, you can release all the items at the same time by using the release code.

11. **How do we release external purchase documents and PRs?**

■ You can release external purchase documents, which include purchasing documents other than PRs, only at the header level. This means that these documents can only be released using the release procedure with classification. You can perform the following steps to release external purchase documents:
  □ Select *Purchasing Document > Release*. The selection screen for the relevant purchasing document appears.
  □ Enter your release code and any other selection criteria.
  □ Select *Program > Execute*.
  □ Select the purchasing document you want to release.
  □ Select *Edit > Release*.
  □ Save the release.
■ You can release PRs using two different procedures:
  □ *Individual release*—Use this if you need to release one item at a time. Follow these steps to perform individual release of PRs:
    ■ Select *Purchase Requisition > Release > Individual Release*.

- Enter the PR number and your release code.
- Press Enter. This opens an overview of the item chosen. You can make changes, if required.
- Select *Go To > Release Info > Release Options*.
- Select the item you want to release and select *Edit > Release > Set*. This releases the selected item.

You should note here that if the item belongs to a complete PR, the releasing item will release all the other related items.

- Save the release.

  □ *Collective release*—You can release all the items by using the release code. Follow these steps to perform collective release of PRs:

  - Select *Requisition > Release > Collective Release*. This opens the selection screen collective release.
  - Enter you release code.
  - Select *Program > Execute*.
  - Select *Edit > Select > Select All*.
  - Save the release.

12. What is a "release criterion"?

- The release criterion defines the strategy by which a PR or an external purchase document is released. The release criteria contains the characteristics and the values of the characteristics, which determine the status of the document, that is, either blocked or not blocked (a characteristic can be the total value of the document, say greater than $100,000). The criterion can be based on any one of or a combination of the following:

  □ Account assignment category
  □ Material group
  □ Plant
  □ Total value

13.   What is the release code?

- The release code is a two-character field or ID that represents the person responsible for the approval of the release procedure.

14.   What is the release group?

- The release group is a two-digit code that is assigned to a class and contains one or more release strategies. For example, release group 01 is defined for PRs and release group 02 is defined for POs.

GLOSSARY

Accounting document
Accounting documents are the type of documents that are prepared if goods movements influence the financial accounting.

Batch information cockpit
The batch information cockpit (BIC) is the main switching point and has a wide range of options for scrutiny and control. It combines the views and analysis of batch information at a single location.

Batch
A batch is a group of materials put together quantity-wise for various reasons. Materials with the same characteristics and values are often grouped into a batch.

Class
A class is a collection of a group of characteristics for a particular object.

Client
A client can be defined as a person, company, or organization that purchases and pays for goods from another person, company, or organization. In SAP, a client can be defined as a self-contained unit that has its own master records and set of tables.

Company
A company is an organizational unit for which individual financial statements are drawn as per the relevant commercial laws. A company consists of one or more company codes.

Consignment
Consignment is the act of storing materials at some other premises but holding the ownership of the materials until the materials are sold or shifted elsewhere.

Consumption-based planning

Consumption-based planning (CBP) is a method of planning based on past consumption of materials and is used to forecast future material requirements.

Contract

A contract is an agreement between a customer and a vendor that states that the vendor will supply materials to the customer at an agreed price within a specified period of time.

Document management system

A document management system (DMS) in SAP stores external documents such as goods or materials pictures.

Dunning

Dunning is a payment reminder or notice sent to a business partner for the payment of outstanding debts.

Evaluated receipt settlement

Evaluated receipt settlement (ERS) is the procedure for settling goods receipts automatically. It is a process in which the goods receipt and the purchase order are matched and then posted without an invoice.

Forecast-based planning

In this type of materials resource planning (MRP), the forecast values and the future requirements for the material are determined by a forecasting program.

FRC

The FRC is a type of SA release. You can use the FRC delivery schedules to provide a medium-term overview about your requirements.

Goods issue reversal

The goods issue reversal is entered on the basis of the material document that was created upon the initial goods issue, or on the basis of a reservation made for stock for the production order.

Goods issue

Goods issue refers to the physical movement of goods or material out of the company.

Goods receipt

Goods receipt is the process in which material is received from a vendor or from the in-house production process. There are other types of goods receipt in SAP including initial stock creation.

Inventory management

Inventory management in the SAP system provides the client with very effective processes for all types of goods movements within the plant. The effective streamlining of plant processes can help companies reduce order-to-delivery time, reduce costs, decrease inventory, and enhance customer service.

Invoice verification

Invoice verification is the process of checking the accuracy of an invoice in terms of the quantity, price, and other related information.

Just-in-time (JIT) delivery

JIT delivery is a type of SA release that you can use to schedule and inform the vendor of your requirements for the near future.

Logistics invoice verification (LIV)

LIV is a part of materials management (MM). It is the last component of the logistics supply chain comprised of purchasing, inventory management, and invoice verification. In invoice verification, vendor invoices are compared with respect to purchase orders and goods receipts.

Master data

Master data is the data that is permanent for the materials in the SAP system.

Material master records

Material master records are used in the SAP R/3 system to manage material-specific data. Material information stored in material master records is used by all logistics areas in the SAP R/3 system.

Materials requirement planning (MRP)

MRP guarantees procurement and production of the required quantities of materials on time, whether the material is required for internal purposes or for sales and distribution.

Outline agreement

The outline agreement refers to a deal between the purchasing organization and the vendor to deliver materials or services. The outline agreement also contains all the terms and conditions to be followed at the time of the transaction.

Outline purchase agreement

An outline purchase agreement is a long-term agreement between the purchasing department and a vendor for the supply of materials and services for a given period of time.

Parked invoice document

In a parked invoice document, you can enter the invoice data or the credit memo data into the computer system and save it.

Physical inventory count

Physical inventory count is a count of stock that is currently in stock at a plant or storage location.

Planned order

A planned order is sent to a plant for the procurement of a particular material at a given time.

Plant

A plant is an organizational unit where materials are produced or goods and services are provided.

Procurement

Procurement is the purchase of products, goods, or services at the optimum possible total cost in the correct amount and quality. It is the process of acquiring goods and works, covering both acquisitions from third parties and from in-house providers.

Purchase order (PO)

A PO is a formal request for materials or services from an outside vendor or plant.

Purchase requisition (PR)

A PR is an internal purchasing document that notifies the department, such as purchasing and procurement, to supply goods or services.

Purchasing document

A purchasing document is a document type used by the purchasing department to procure materials or services.

Purchasing information record

The purchasing information record, also known as the info record, contains information relating to a specific material and a vendor supplying this material. It also contains information about the vendor's current price for the material.

Purchasing organization

A purchasing organization is an organizational unit that procures materials and services and negotiates with vendors to purchase materials or goods.

Purchasing value key

A purchasing value key is the key that determines the following: the reminder keys, the under the delivery tolerance limit and over the delivery tolerance limit, and order acknowledgement requirements in the purchase order.

Quotation

A quotation is given to a purchasing organization by a vendor and contains the conditions regarding the supply of materials or performance of services. A quotation is a legal document that binds the vendor for a certain period.

Reorder point planning

Reorder point planning is the planning of MRP stock, where the procurement is triggered when the sum of plant stock and firmed receipts falls below the reorder point.

Request for quotation (RFQ)

An RFQ is a document sent to a vendor by a purchasing organization, to which the vendor responds by sending quotations with prices.

SAP

Systems, Applications, and Products in Data Processing (SAP) is an Enterprise Resource Planning (ERP) software application that provides complete business solutions by integrating various business tasks, such as sales, purchase, and production.

Scheduling agreement (SA)
An SA is an outline purchase agreement between the purchasing department and the vendor containing delivery quantities and dates.

Special stocks
Special stocks are the stocks that must be managed separately by a company.

Stochastic blocking
Stochastic blocking is the process of checking the incoming invoices. In this process, invoices are blocked randomly. Invoices with high value have the highest probability of being blocked.

Stock in transit
Stock in transit is the stock that is removed from the issuing plant but has not yet arrived at the receiving plant.

Stock transport order (STO)
An STO is a purchase order used to transport material from one plant to another within the same corporate enterprise.

Storage location
A storage location is an organizational unit where the goods produced in the plant are stored.

Subcontracting
Subcontracting is the processing of materials by an external supplier.

Time-phased planning
Time-phased planning is an MRP procedure in which the delivery of materials is planned at particular time intervals.

Vendor master data
Vendor master data is all of the details about each of the vendors that supply an enterprise. The vendor master data is stored in individual vendor master records, with each record containing the vendor's name and address. In addition, it contains data such as the currency used for the transaction, payment terms, and the name of the contact person on the sales staff.

Vendor sub-range
The vendor sub-range is a subdivision of the total range of products that a vendor provides. The total range of products is divided into sub-ranges, depending on several criteria, including specification of which material belongs to which vendor sub-range in the vendor's info record.

QUESTION INDEX

Chapter 1: Introduction to SAP Materials Management

1. What is SAP? How is it used in industries?   3
2. Briefly describe the history of the SAP software.   3
3. Why is SAP so popular? What are some of the other ERP applications available in the market?   4
4. What is mySAP ERP? What business components can it by classified into?   5
5. What are the industry-specific solutions available in mySAP?   6
6. What is SAP R/3?   6
7. How did different versions of SAP evolve?   7
8. Why are industry-specific solutions used in SAP R/3?   7
9. What benefits will be realized after implementing SAP in any organization?   8
10. What are the different modules in SAP R/3?   9
11. What are the core functionalities of the SAP system?   10
12. How can we define an MM module? What is its importance in SAP R/3?   10
13. How is the MM module integrated with other modules of SAP?   10
14. What are the main components of the MM module? How are these components used in SAP?   11

Chapter 2: Organizational Structure

1. What is the organizational structure in the materials management (MM) module? 15
2. What are the levels of organizational units in Enterprise Structure in SAP R/3? 16
3. Define "client". What is its importance in SAP? 16
4. How do we create a client in the MM module? 16
5. Define "company". How is it different from a client? What are the data in the MM module that are maintained at the company code level? 17
6. How do we create a company code in SAP? 17
7. How do we assign a company code to a company in SAP? 18
8. How many charts of accounts can be assigned to a company? 18
9. How many company codes can be assigned to one chart of accounts? 18
10. How many company codes can be assigned to a company? 18
11. What is a plant in the MM module? 18
12. How is a plant defined in the MM module? 19
13. What are the prerequisites for creating a plant? 19
14. How many company codes can be assigned to a plant? 20
15. Can a company code be assigned to many plants? 20
16. What is the menu path to assign a company code to a plant? 20
17. What is a storage location in SAP? 20
18. How is storage location defined in SAP? 20
19. How is a storage location assigned to a plant? 21
20. Can storage locations be created automatically? 21
21. Can two plants have a common storage location? 21
22. What is the menu path to configure the storage location? 22
23. What is a purchasing organization in SAP? 22
24. What are the different ways of organizing purchasing organizations? 22
25. How is a purchasing organization defined in SAP? 22
26. What is the reference purchasing organization in SAP? 23
27. How is a purchase group defined in SAP? 23

Chapter 3: Master Data

1. What is master data in the materials management (MM) module? 27
2. How is master data important in the MM module? 27
3. What are the various types of master data in the MM module? 27
4. What is a material master file? 28
5. Why are material master records used in SAP? 28
6. How is the information in material master records updated? 28
7. What are the types of industry sectors defined in the material master data? 28
8. What data in the material master is maintained at the client level? 29
9. What data in the material master is maintained at the company code level? 29
10. What are the plant-specific data in the material master? 29
11. What is the lot size attribute of a material? 29
12. How is material information structured in material master records? 30
13. What is a batch? 30
14. Why is a batch record important? 30
15. How do we create a batch? 30
16. What are the important fields in a batch master record? 31
17. How can batch records be changed? 31
18. How do we delete a batch? 32
19. What is the Batch Information Cockpit? 32
20. What are the levels at which a batch number can be configured? 32
21. How are batch numbers assigned? 33
22. What is a serial number? 33
23. What is a class type? How do we configure a class type? 33
24. How can we procure a master record for a material that does not have one? 34
25. What is the importance of classification data? 34
26. What is an ABC indicator? 34
27. What are the main master files used in MM? 35
28. Give some examples of master data in MM. 35
29. How do we create a vendor? 35
30. What is vendor master data? 35

31. What are the different sections in vendor master data?   36
32. What are the different fields in vendor master data?   36
33. How do we create a vendor number range?   36
34. What is dunning procedure? How can it be configured?   37
35. How do we assign material to vendors?   37
36. What is the transaction code to access the Materials Management Configuration menu?   37
37. What are the various transaction codes to access the MM configuration?   38
38. Write the names of some important MM tables.   38
39. What are purchasing information records?   39
40. What are the categories of purchasing information records?   39
41. What are the prerequisites for creating a purchasing info record?   39
42. How can we create a purchasing info record?   40
43. Can a purchasing info record be created without a material number?   40
44. How can we create an information record based on the material master?   40
45. What is the document management system (DMS) in SAP?   41
46. What is the document information record?   41
47. How does one create a document?   42
48. What are the key fields that one must specify when creating a document?   42
49. How does one link a document to a material master record?   42
50. How will you link a document to a vendor master record?   42
51. How is the classification system used to describe a document?   43
52. How can material numbers be assigned in a material master file?   43
53. What data is contained in the information record?   43
54. How do we change the standard price in the material master?   44
55. What is the source of the "not allowed" error in the case of custom movement type creation?   44
56. Give the names of the tables where the header level and item data are stored in a purchase order.   44
57. Give the names of the tables where the material master data is stored.   44

58. What is the vendor evaluation? How is it maintained?   44
59. List the components of the master data and their transaction codes.   45
60. What is the name of the SAP program used to update or create material master records?   45
61. What is storage location-specific material master data?   45
62. When is a production resource/tool (PRT) defined for a material?   45
63. What transaction code is used to extend the material view?   46
64. Give some examples of information related to a material's storage and warehousing.   46
65. What is a source list? What is the menu path to define a source list?   46
66. How do we create a source list?   46
67. What is the transaction code for creating a source list?   46
68. What transaction codes are used with a source list and what is their purpose?   47
69. What are material numbers in SAP?   47
70. What does an industry sector control?   47
71. Can we change the industry sector of an existing material?   47
72. What is the material type of a material?   48
73. What is a valuation category?   48
74. What does the material type control?   49
75. What is the transaction code to create a material type?   49
76. What are the general material types used in SAP?   49
77. What material types are used while creating a new material?   50
78. What is the menu path to define material type attributes?   50
79. Can we change the material type of a material?   51
80. What is the shelf life expiration date check? Where is it maintained?   51
81. How do we set user defaults for views?   51
82. List the steps to create a profile.   51
83. How do we change the characteristics?   52
84. How do we create a class?   52
85. Can we include an ROH type in the sales view?   52
86. List the key fields of the material master table.   52
87. What are the major purchasing tables? List the transaction codes for them.   52
88. What is nonvaluated material?   53

89. What are the views in material master? Which data, in general, do these views contain?   53

90. What are the fields in a material master file?   54

91. What are the important fields in the Basic Data view?   56

92. How can we access the additional data screen?   56

93. What are the important fields in the Accounting view?   57

94. What are the important fields in sales organization data?   57

95. What are the important fields in plant data?   58

96. What are the important fields in the Purchasing view?   59

97. How can we create a material in SAP?   60

98. What does "extending a material" mean? How is this done?   62

99. How can we create a material master record?   64

100. How can we change a material master record?   66

101. List the steps to delete a material master record.   67

102. How can we display the material master record on the SAP system?   68

103. How do we move a material master record from one SAP system to another?   69

104. What is the transaction code to display material in SAP MM?   69

105. What is the purchasing value key?   69

106. How can we configure the purchasing value key?   69

107. Define "material group".   70

108. Define "material status".   70

109. What is the base unit of measure of a material? What are the other units of measure used in SAP for a material?   70

110. How do we create a vendor master record?   71

111. How can we change a vendor master record?   72

112. How can we block a vendor?   73

113. What is the vendor subrange?   74

114. What is a one-time vendor?   74

Chapter 4: Procurement and Purchasing

1. What are the special stocks used in materials management (MM)?   77

2. What are the differences between company-owned special stocks and externally-owned special stocks?   78

3. Why do organizations need negative stock?   78

4. What are special procurement types?   78

5. Define "consignment stock". What are the main features of consignment stock?   79

6. How is the pricing of consignment stocks done? What information does the consignment information record contain?   80

7. How are consignment stocks created?   80

8. Define "consignment cycle".   80

9. How is consignment material procured?   80

10. How can we see the consignment stocks in SAP?   81

11. How can we take consignment stocks into our own stock?   81

12. Can we do the physical inventory check of consignment stocks?   81

13. How can we invoice in the case of consignment stocks?   82

14. What is subcontracting?   82

15. How is subcontracting used in MM?   82

16. What information does the subcontracting info record contain?   82

17. How do we create a subcontracting purchase order (PO)?   83

18. How can we view the stocks provided to a vendor?   84

19. How are components (materials) provided to the vendor?   84

20. How are components consumed in subcontracting?   84

21. Why do we need to create physical inventory documents for an inventory cycle-count procedure of a material or materials?   85

22. What is the difference between planned and unplanned consumption?   85

23. How can we provide components to the vendor or subcontractor with and without a PO reference?   85

24. How can one vendor obtain components from another vendor or third party?   86

25. How do we verify invoices for subcontracting POs?   86

26. How do we attach a document to the PO?   87

27. How do we know if the PO has been issued?   87

28. How can we create a subcontract order?   87

29. What is STO? What are its advantages?   87

30. Is the goods receipt/invoice receipt (GR/IR) account needed in inventory?   88

31. How is stock transfer done between the plants? What are one-step and two-step stock transfer?   88

32. Define "lot size".   89

33. What is a reservation?   89

34. What transaction codes are used with reservations?   90

35. How is the list of all reservations in the systems displayed?   90

36. What is the difference between stock transfer and transfer posting?   90

37. What is the transaction code to create movement types?   90

38. How can we create movement types?   90

39. Why is the stock transfer order set up in the initial configuration?   91

40. How is stock transferred with and without delivery?   91

41. How is stock transferred in a cross-company scenario?   92

42. How can we post a goods issue in the case of an STO?   92

43. How can we monitor stock in transit?   93

44. How is a goods receipt entered in the receiving plant in the case of an STO?   94

45. How can a stock transfer be monitored in Purchasing?   94

46. How is an STO created?   95

47. Define "source list".   95

48. How do we generate a source list?   95

49. What are the different source determination procedures?   96

50. How does source determination work in the case of purchase requisitions?   96

51. What are purchase requisitions as related to SAP?   97

52. How can a purchase requisition be created?   97

53. How can we create a purchase requisition with a material master record?   98

54. Can we generate a purchase requisition automatically?   99

55. How can we create a purchase requisition without a material master record?   99

56. How do we track a purchase requisition?   100

57. When can a purchase requisition be closed?   100

58. State the configuration steps for a purchase requisition.   101

59. What are the important fields in a purchase requisition?   101

60. How do we change a purchase requisition once it is issued?   101

61. State the differences between the purchase requisition with a master record and without a master record.   102

62. State the importance of the vendor evaluation in the purchase department?   102

63. What are the main criteria of the vendor evaluation?   102

64. How do we maintain the vendor evaluations in the MM module?   103

65. What are the document types used in purchase requisitions?   103

66. What is the difference between an indirectly created and directly created purchase requisition?   103

67. Can a purchase requisition be manually generated through the reference of a PO or a scheduling agreement?   103

68. What is a PO? What does a PO contain?   104

69. Where do we define payment terms in the PO?   104

70. What are the document types used in a PO?   104

71. What is the difference between a blanket PO and a service order?   104

72. What is price comparison?   104

73. What are the document types used in scheduling agreements?   105

74. What are the document types used in a contract?   105

75. What is a contract?   105

76. What are the different types of contracts?   105

77. What is the difference between a scheduling agreement and a contract?   106

78. How can we create a contract?   106

79. Account assignment categories "U" and "X" can be used in purchase requisitions but not in POs. Why?   106

80. What is the difference in release procedure between internal documents and external documents?   107

81. Define "procurement cycle".   107

82. What are the main documents used in MM?   109

83. What are the various steps of the MM cycle?   109

84. What is the definition of procurement?   109

85. What is the account assignment category in a PO document?   110

86. What is the difference between a PO and a purchase requisition?   110

87. What is the creation indicator?   110

88. What is the automatic generation of POs from purchase requisitions?   110

89. What is a quotation?   111

90. How do we enter a quotation from a vendor in the SAP system?   111

91. How can we compare price factors in quotations?   111

92. What are the qualitative factors that can prove advantageous to the client while bidding?   112

93. How can we reject a quotation?   113

94. What is an RFQ?   113

95. How are RFQs and quotations processed in SAP?   114

96. How can an RFQ be created?   114

97. What transaction codes are used in RFQs?   115

98. How can we create an RFQ in the SAP system?   115

99. What is the RFQ type?   115

100. List the important key fields for RFQs.   115

101. What is the RFQ delivery schedule?   116

102. How can we release an RFQ?   116

103. What is the purchasing document category for an RFQ?   116

104. How can we find the list of vendors to send an RFQ?   116

105. What is the role of the confirmation control key?   116

106. What is a purchasing document?   117

107. What are the various transactions codes used in Materials Management Purchasing (MM-PUR)?   117

108. Name some of the data points provided by purchasing for the materials.   117

109. What are the external purchasing documents available in the standard SAP system?   118

110. How does the SAP system differentiate between purchasing documents?   118

111. How are purchasing documents numbered?   118

112. What is meant by PO, as related to SAP? What are the different ways a PO can be created in SAP?   119

113. How can we create a PO automatically?   120

114. How can we create POs with known and unknown vendors?   120

115. Can a line item in a PO be blocked after it has been created?   121

116. How can we cancel a PO line item?   121

117. What are the account assignment categories in a PO?   121

118. Can multiple accounts be assigned to a PO line?   121

119. What is an outline purchase agreement? What are the types of outline purchase agreements?   121

120. What is an item category? What will happen if we use the consignment item category in SAP? What will happen if we use the subcontracting item category in a PO?   122

121. What are the different types of item category?   122

122. What is an account assignment category? How is it configured?   123

123. What is a scheduling agreement? How can it be created?   123

124. How can we create a scheduling agreement with a reference?   123

125. What are the allowed account assignment categories in a PO?   124
126. What is service procurement?   124
127. What is the mandatory data that we must enter while creating a PO?   124
128. Where can we maintain the conditions in the PO?   125
129. What is the difference between procurement for stock and procurement for consumption?   125
130. What is the difference between external procurement and internal procurement?   126
131. What is a document type?   126
132. What are the ways of converting planned orders into purchase requisitions?   126
133. What transaction code is used to convert planned orders into requisitions in MRP?   126
134. Can we add custom fields to POs and RFQs?   127
135. What are the external purchasing documents and internal purchasing documents used in MM?   127
136. How is a framework order (FO) different from a standard PO?   127
137. What document types can be used in cases of service procurement?   127
138. What is the procurement type? What are the procurement types used in SAP?   128
139. Why should we use multiple account assignment in a PO?   128
140. How is the Stock Transport Order (STO) different from the standard PO?   128
141. How can we return a material that we have received with reference to a PO?   129
142. How are free items managed in a PO?   129
143. Which documents are used as references when we create a PO?   129
144. Suppose we want to procure a material using a PO and intend to accept delivery of the material at different times. In addition, if such material has a graduated discount scale, how would we proceed to take advantage of the discount arrangement?   129
145. Explain the significance of the PO price unit. In addition, what should we note in case of a goods receipt?   130
146. What is the transaction code to set price control for receipts (goods/invoice)?   130

147. What is the outline agreement? What is the difference between a contract and a scheduling agreement?   130
148. What is the difference between quantity and value contracts?   131
149. What is a centrally agreed contract?   131
150. What is a service master record?   132
151. List the important fields of a service master record.   132
152. What is a standard service catalog (SSC)?   132
153. How can the services be purchased?   132
154. What is a service entry sheet?   133
155. What is a blanket PO? How can it be created?   133
156. What is a distributed contract?   133
157. What are the allowed item categories used with contracts?   134
158. How can we create a scheduling agreement in SAP?   134
159. What are schedule lines?   134
160. How can we create a schedule line in for a scheduling agreement?   135
161. How is a scheduling agreement release sent to a vendor?   136
162. Define FRC and JIT.   136
163. Define "firm" and "trade-off zone".   137
164. Define "creation profile".   137
165. What does the document type control? How are purchase requisition document types linked with PO and RFQ document types?   138
166. What is tax code?   139

Chapter 5: Materials Requirement Planning

1. What is materials requirement planning (MRP) in SAP?   143
2. List the types of MRP.   143
3. What MRP procedures are available in consumption-based planning (CBP)?   144
4. What is the MRP list?   144
5. What are the different transaction codes used for different activities in CBP?   144
6. What is CBP and how can we integrate it?   145
7. What is the difference between MRP and CBP?   146

8. What important values are used to define the reorder point?   146
9. What is a procurement proposal? What are the types of procurement proposals?   146
10. What is reorder point planning?   146
11. How is the automatic purchase order generated using a particular material after creation of a purchase requistion?   147
12. What is forecasting in the SAP system?   148
13. What are the different models for forecasting?   148
14. Can the forecast model be selected automatically?   149
15. What are the fields in forecast profile creation?   149
16. What is forecast-based planning?   150
17. What are the different types of forecast model?   150
18. Define "time-phased planning".   150
19. Define "planning process flow".   151
20. Define "planning run type".   151
21. Define "planning calendars".   152
22. How can we create a planning calendar in CBP?   152
23. How is planning done at the plant level and storage location level?   152
24. How is the net requirement calculated?   153
25. How is the lot-size calculation performed in MRP?   154
26. What are static lot-sizing procedures?   155
27. What is a rounding profile?   155
28. How is scheduling carried out in MRP?   155
29. What is the difference between backward scheduling and forward scheduling?   156
30. What are the basic types of model selection?   156
31. How is the procurement type determined?   156
32. What is the use of the special procurement type?   157
33. How does the system automatically determine the source of supply?   157
34. What is meant by the term "confirmation control key"?   158
35. What is the MRP area?   159
36. What are the control parameters for planning runs?   159
37. Define "creation indicators".   160
38. What are the conditions required to create the planned orders?   161
39. What is the transaction code to convert planned orders into purchase requisitions?   161

40. What is total planning? 161
41. How is the procurement proposal created through MRP? 161
42. Define "planned order". How is it created? 162
43. How is a planned order converted into a purchase requisition? 163
44. Define "planning time fence". 164
45. How can we disable a reservation in MRP? 164

Chapter 6: Inventory Management

1. Give an overview of inventory management in the SAP system. 167
2. What tasks are covered under inventory management? 167
3. What is physical inventory? 167
4. What are the initial configuration steps for purchase acquisition? 168
5. What is the difference between managing stock by quantity and managing stock by value? 168
6. What are "special stocks" in SAP? 169
7. With which modules in SAP is inventory management integrated? 169
8. How is inventory management integrated with the MM module? 170
9. What are the initial configuration steps for inventory management? 170
10. What is "goods movement"? What types of documents are created after goods movement? 170
11. What are the goods movements that take place in the MM module? 171
12. What are "goods receipt" and "goods issue"? 172
13. Why is goods receipt important to a company? 172
14. How is a goods receipt performed? 173
15. How do you post the goods if the purchase order number is not known? 173
16. How is the vendor return processed without a purchase order reference? 173
17. What happens when a goods receipt is posted? 173
18. What are the types of goods receipts that cannot be received through normal procedures? How do we receive these goods? 174

19. How can a goods receipt be posted when the purchase order number is unknown?   175
20. What are the results of goods movements?   175
21. How do we receive goods from production?   175
22. What documents are created with goods movement?   175
23. How is a material document cancelled?   176
24. How can we find the logical value of stock items?   177
25. What are the ways of receiving goods?   177
26. What is the movement type?   177
27. What does a movement type control?   178
28. What is a planned goods receipt?   178
29. What is goods receipt blocked stock? How is a material received in goods also received in blocked stock?   178
30. List the movement types for unplanned goods received.   179
31. What are the ways through which we can receive goods without a reference?   179
32. How is a return delivery posted in the sales documents?   180
33. How can an item be returned to a vendor?   180
34. What is goods issue reversal?   180
35. What are the documents that are created when a goods issue is posted?   181
36. What are the results of the goods issue?   181
37. Where is the goods issue performed?   182
38. How can we perform the goods issue in SAP?   182
39. What are goods issues to a production order, to scrap, and for sampling?   183
40. How is a goods issue done in SAP?   183
41. How is a material scrapped?   184
42. What is availability check?   184
43. How do we create a return delivery to the vendor?   185
44. What is a stock transfer?   186
45. What are the different ways of making a stock transfer?   187
46. What is a transfer posting?   187
47. How is stock transferred from one storage location to another?   188
48. How is stock transferred from one plant to another plant?   188
49. How is stock transferred from company code to company code?   188
50. What is material-to-material transfer?   189

51. How is stock transferred and posted using the stock determination functions?   189

52. How are the material documents for stock transfer created?   189

53. State the difference between the one-step and two-step procedures in stock transfer.   190

54. What is meant by the term "reservation"?   190

55. What is the purpose of a reservation?   191

56. What is physical inventory?   192

57. What is stock posting?   192

58. How is the value of cross-company-code stock displayed?   192

59. Describe the process of physical inventory count.   192

60. How can we prepare the inventory count difference list in SAP?   193

61. How can we post a count document?   193

62. How can we post a count in the SAP system without a physical count document?   193

63. How are inventory differences accounted for?   194

64. Define the process of creating the physical inventory.   194

65. What are the special stocks in inventory management?   195

66. What are externally-owned special stocks?   196

67. Define "procurement types".   196

68. Name the documents posted during goods movements in inventory management and list the codes.   197

69. How is vendor consignment useful?   198

70. What is returnable transport packaging (RTP)?   198

71. What is sales order stock?   198

72. What is project stock?   198

Chapter 7: Logistics Invoice Verification

1. What does the term LIV mean?   201

2. What are the main features of LIV?   202

3. What is invoice verification?   202

4. What are the different types of invoice verification?   202

5. What is the transaction code for invoice verification?   202

6. How can we perform invoice verification?   202

7. How can we process an invoice verification?   203

8. What are the main steps in the invoice verification process?   205

9. Define ERS.   206
10. Invoice verification is done with reference to which documents?   206
11. What is a parked invoice document?   206
12. How do we park an invoice?   207
13. What is the benefit of document parking?   208
14. How do we display the parked document?   208
15. What is posting an invoice? How is it different from parking an invoice?   208
16. What is a credit memo?   208
17. What are subsequent debit and subsequent credit?   209
18. Define "invoice status".   209
19. What is stochastic blocking?   210
20. How can we manually block an invoice?   210
21. What is total-based invoice reduction?   211
22. What are the different accounts used in invoicing?   211
23. How do we enter the planned delivery cost in an invoice?   211
24. How are quantity and price variances entered?   212
25. How do we post an invoice?   213
26. What are the different types of variances in invoices? Describe them.   215
27. Why do invoices get blocked?   215
28. What happens when an invoice is blocked? What are the different ways to block an invoice?   215
29. How do we release an invoice?   216
30. How can we post an invoice directly without any references?   216
31. How does the SAP system validate the data of an incoming invoice?   216
32. What do the W, V, and F fields show in the status of a document in FBV3?   218
33. What is the menu path to create a document or e-mail notification for your supplier?   218
34. What are invoice tolerances? How can we post small differences?   218
35. What is the difference between GR-based IV and PO-based IV?   218
36. What are the planned delivery costs involved in purchasing?   219
37. How are taxes posted at the time of invoice verification?   219

Chapter 8: Valuation and Account Assignment

1. How can we create the vendor account group in SAP? 223
2. What is the purpose of material valuation? 223
3. How do we determine the stock value? 223
4. How is material valuation associated with financial accounting? 224
5. What factors control material valuation? 224
6. What is the valuation area? 224
7. What is the difference between the valuation area at the company code level and at the plant level? 224
8. Define "valuation class". 224
9. How is a valuation class configured? 225
10. Explain material valuation with the moving average price. 225
11. Explain material valuation with the standard price. 226
12. What is the valuation level in the SAP system? 226
13. What is the significance of an account assignment category? 226
14. What are the account assignment categories? 227
15. How can we create a purchase requisition with single and multiple account assignments? 227
16. How can we create a purchase order with reference to a purchase requisition with an account assignment? 227
17. How can we maintain account assignment categories in the SAP system? 228
18. What is the balance sheet valuation? 228
19. What is a LIFO valuation? 228
20. How can we configure a LIFO valuation? 229
21. What is a FIFO valuation? 230
22. Briefly describe the types by which a material value is determined. 230
23. What is the importance of the material ledger? 230
24. What are the ways in which the material price can be determined? 231

Chapter 9: Release Procedures

1. What is the release procedure? 235
2. What is the release strategy? How many release points can be involved in a release process? 235

3. Can you release the PO item by item when you have a
   multi-line-item PO?   235
4. How are the release procedures for PRs and POs
   defined?   236
5. How are the release procedures configured?   236
6. How do we release blocked purchase documents?   236
7. How do we reject approvals in the SAP R/3 system? Will it
   affect the SAP business workflow?   236
8. How many procedures are available to release PRs?   236
9. How do we release POs? Which transaction code is used to
   display as well as reset the release of POs?   237
10. How many types of release procedures are available for
    POs?   237
11. How do we release external purchase documents and
    PRs?   237
12. What is a "release criterion"?   238
13. What is the release code?   239
14. What is the release group?   239